ALBERT CAMUS AND THE MINISTER

Albert Camus
and the Minister

Howard Mumma

PARACLETE PRESS
BREWSTER, MASSACHUSETTS

Library of Congress Cataloging-in-Publication Data

Mumma, Howard E.
    Albert Camus and the minister / Howard Mumma.
        p. cm.
Includes bibliographical references.
    ISBN 1-55725-246-7 (pbk.)
    1. Mumma, Howard E.—Friends and associates. 2. Camus, Albert,
1913-1960. I. Title.
    BX8495.M86 A3 2000
    287'.6'092—dc21   00-008354

10 9 8 7 6 5 4 3 2 1

© 2000 by Howard Mumma
ISBN 1–55725–246–7

Brewster, Massachusetts
www.paracletepress.com

Printed in the United States of America.

For Elizabeth—
my wife, best friend and
companion for fifty-eight years,
and I hope for many years
to come.

Table of Contents

THE MINISTER—
HEROES AND FRIENDS

LESSONS

Acknowledgments

When I first made notes on the people who have influenced and enriched my life, I had no intention of putting any of the contents into a book. It has been only in the past two years that I began to compile this manuscript.

I owe a special debt of gratitude to all the people who by their friendly comments and questions encouraged me. To my friend George Hall, I owe an unpayable debt; his editorial work is largely responsible for whatever value and interest these essays and conversations may have.

I also thank our daughter, Katharine Baker, for her help.

I wish to express my appreciation to Lillian Miao, Ph.D., CEO of Paraclete Press, for her help and encouragement through out the preparation of this manuscript for publication.

Thanks also go to Janette Taylor for her typing.

Introduction

My fifty-nine years as a minister have taught me that preaching has severe limitations. From the pulpit, I have learned the hard way that teaching is a much better way to equip people to live their lives to the fullest. Wherever the opportunity presented itself—in the pulpit, the classroom, the counseling room, or even across the table over lunch—I have always tried to combine teaching and counseling as the situation warranted. This book relates how I worked at this.

To this end, I will describe the dialogues I had with two gifted writers—Albert Camus and Jean-Paul Sartre. Both writers rejected the very existence of God, much less the idea of a loving, caring God. I was put to the test in an attempt to bring each of them to a better understanding of the divine nature of God.

I occasionally fell back on preaching, but I did my best to teach and counsel. Despite their congruence of nihilistic atheism, they differed markedly in psychological makeup. Camus was much more of a soul searcher, looking for meaning beyond himself, and willing to give and take. His novels and other writings touch the soul, for me anyway, as deeply and profoundly as Dostoyevsky. By contrast, Sartre was more the dogmatist. He, probably, was stronger in intellectual power and did not lack in pride, but then again neither do I.

I will never forget these two men. In my mind, it seems as if it were only last year that I talked to them. But, while the intensity of the experience endures, my memory of the exact words does not, nor can I vouch for perfect translation from French, when that was the case. I did not go to the extreme of creating a midrash, as a midrash is justified only when the historical record is tauntingly inadequate and traces no living memory of events past. I am, however, probably guilty of hagiography arising from a not-so-clear recollection of the exact words spoken. After all, these conversations were neither recorded nor transcribed, although I did make a few notes after each meeting. This is somewhat like the so-called synoptic Gospels (Matthew, Mark, and Luke), which were all written down from oral tradition and some after-the-fact written notes. Not surprisingly, these three Gospels differ markedly in the words spoken by Christ and his contemporaries. Moreover, the accounts of the events and their sequence lack consistency. Yet, all three tell essentially the same story. Likewise, I hope my transgressions in exact wording used do not intrude upon the spirit of our conversations.

Lastly, I am not letting you off the hook with just the account of my conversations with Albert Camus and Jean-Paul Sartre—far from it. In my travels around the world, I have also had the opportunity to discuss Christianity *vis-à-vis* other great religions of the world with the adherents of those religions. I have tried to delineate some of the things that Christianity and Eastern religions can learn from each other, and to expand on Luther's most famed remark: "Here I stand; there you stand; can we share?"

While in India, I learned that the Buddhists believe that the accumulation of knowledge and characteristics is reformed into new beings in such a way that progress is achieved. Nothing is lost. I like that—the lesson is clear. In our formative years, we are each bequeathed the accumulated storehouse of scientific knowledge and technological prowess. But, we have to ask if the same progress in spiritual matters can be claimed. We must ask: "Has each generation grown in spirit, drawing on the knowledge and wisdom of its forebears?" I cannot honestly answer that question, but of one thing I am certain—it cannot happen unless each of us makes a point of summarizing the lessons we have learned from life and of passing that summary on for our successors in life to at least consider.

By the time this is published, I will have passed my ninetieth birthday. I want to leave the world a better place than I found it. And if that's not possible, at least I want to pass along something of the legacy I inherited from my parents, my teachers, my parishioners, and my friends.

The American Church in Paris
65, Quai d'Orsay

THE WEARIED EXISTENTIALIST: CONVERSATIONS WITH CAMUS

Author's Note

It's fair to ask why I waited so long to publish this account of my conversations with Camus—and if, after so many years, the account could be accurate. I want to make it clear that I did not have conversations with Albert Camus on a regular basis; our conversations were irregular and occasional, spanning several years. One thing was certain: Every time he requested a meeting, he had something definite on his mind that he wished to discuss.

During our second or third meeting, Camus asked if I might agree that our visits would be kept confidential—that no records of dates of our meetings be kept. "After all," he said, "You are a priest!" I smiled and quickly agreed.

Ministers aren't generally known for reneging on promises, but now, at the age of ninety-one—and with

Camus forty years dead—I am confident that the benefits of sharing his story far outweigh the betrayal of confidence. Fortunately, after each of my conversations with Camus, I returned home and made copious notes. It is from these notes and my memory that I have reconstructed our conversations. This does not mean that the report is verbatim. I am guilty of putting a few words into my acquaintance's mouth—and, for that matter, my own—to better capture the essence of our sessions.

On the other hand, I am not trying to sugarcoat my shortcomings. It is plain to me, that despite how hard I tried, I failed Camus, and the consequences were tragic.

Chapter One

For several summers during the 1950s, I served as guest minister and preacher at the American Church in Paris, on *Quai d'Orsay*. It was the first American church founded on foreign soil and the oldest American institution in Europe. The famous American architect Ralph Adams Cram built the Gothic edifice following World War I. On my first trip to Paris, I found the timeless beauty of the building overwhelming. The design of both the Sanctuary and the educational wing was especially appealing in the use of space, which was efficient and functional. As I first entered the educational wing, I was greeted by the sight of people from all over the United States, and indeed all around the world, gathering, visiting, and laughing happily.

For many foreigners living in Paris, this church was an anchor, a refuge, an escape from the hustle-bustle world, and even a second home. Fine Casavant organ concerts attracted Parisians, students from the Sorbonne, tourists, and Americans of every degree: NATO personnel, members of Congress, and even ambassadors.

During my first weeks at the American Church, I became spoiled by the large attendance. Beginning with my first Sunday as guest minister, a renowned organist by the name of Marcel Dupré played for the services. He was scheduled to play throughout my first month in Paris, and he brought many listeners with him. So when a lesser-known organist replaced him, I counted many empty seats. I reminded myself that the French were not known as avid church-goers and found some consolation in the number of people who did choose to attend. After services, I greeted parishioners on the church steps and thanked each of them for coming.

It was from these steps that I first saw him. He was standing in the midst of a small crowd. Each of the people surrounding him held out a church bulletin to be autographed. His dress separated him from the crowd. Despite the warmth of the June morning, he wore a dark, single-breasted suit, a white shirt, and a dark tie. He was of medium height and build, but walked with a slight stoop. His face was pale with expressive, sad eyes, but the smile he wore while conversing was oddly attractive and charming. When he saw me, he smiled all the more while disengaging himself from the crowd. He walked toward me with his hand raised as if to draw my attention.

"Monsieur, Reverend, thank you, thank you for the service."

"Well, thank you for coming," I said, shaking the offered hand. "Who might you be?"

"I am Albert Camus. I have been here four Sundays and only today did I finally get a seat!" he said with a silent laugh. His face became thoughtful and somber, though, as he spoke again, "For these past Sundays, I came to hear Marcel Dupré play, but today I came to hear you. Would you have lunch with me tomorrow?"

"I would be honored," I said. He seemed pleased, and when we finished making the arrangements, he shook my hand again. "I look forward to our meeting," he said and left as quickly as he had appeared. I was amazed. I had read some of his work. My mind began to search through the many things I had heard concerning this man who had come to this church to hear me preach. Wasn't he a communist? As one of the best known existentialist writers of the day, certainly he was an atheist. I pondered the meaning of the meeting for the rest of the day.

That evening, I ate supper with the church's concierge, Jacques, and his family. Jacques and his wife had been the first people to greet me in Paris. He was a refugee who had been involved in the Spanish Civil War of 1934. He escaped from Spain to France where he changed his name from Juan to Jacques. Jacques told stories about how the socialists and the Popular Front fought against each other in Spain and how it all led up to the second World War. The family invited me to dine with them occasionally, and apparently I was one of the first people at the church to take an interest in them. My interest meant a lot to them, and after an enjoyable meal, I went off to bed contented with my evening.

It was about ten o'clock, but I was far from sleepy. My mind kept returning to the man outside the church, Albert Camus. To me, he was one of the most fascinating Frenchmen of the day. I wondered how formal our lunch would be. Would he be able to understand my English? I certainly knew little French. What could a Christian minister from the United States, a guest preacher, at that, possibly have in common with this great existentialist?

Existentialism, I knew, came from the word "existence," and was a response to the challenge of finding meaning in a seemingly absurd world. According to what I knew of Camus and his contemporary, Jean-Paul Sartre, existentialists believe that we cannot explain the essence of man in the same way that we explain an article of manufacture. For example, we know that a spoon was made by someone who first had its idea—a vision of what the spoon would be used for and how it would be made. Even before the spoon was constructed, the intention was fated with a definite purpose. That is to say, we conceived of the spoon's purpose and method of manufacture, its essence, before it was actually created. Hence, essence preceded existence.

Christians think of a man in much the same way, believing that he was first conceived by God and then created. Existentialists, for the most part, reject God. Instead, they believe that man simply existed. As a result of this existence, man had to confront himself and his experiences in order to define himself and his purpose. In other words, his existence preceded his essence. In blunt terms, each man became his own god.

As I pondered existentialism and its implications, I began to wonder if Camus would try to convert me to his point of view. The conversion of a minister would perhaps be a great feat for him. I could think of no other sensible motivation for his desire to speak to me. My only recourse was to go to sleep and patiently await my lunch with this great writer.

He arrived for me at exactly one o'clock, in a convertible, again wearing a dark, double-breasted suit. He brought another man with him who he said had a better grasp of English, should language be a problem. After collecting me, he drove down the Orleáns road through farmland to a small restaurant. "We will not be bothered here," he said with a slight smirk. "The owners know that I will never come back if they advertise my presence."

The building was set amid open fields with cement walls that gave it the look of a miniature castle. There was only a small wood-burned plaque above the door to tell you that this was a place of business. When we were seated, I ordered a salad and onion soup. Camus ordered a veal chop. During lunch he asked me a bit about myself. I told him that I graduated from Yale College and Yale Divinity School. I told him that, after ordination, I had moved back to Ohio to be a minister and now lived there with my wife and three daughters. He smiled at my comments and nodded, listening intently. Then he asked more questions.

When we had finished our meal, Camus clasped his hands on the table and suddenly turned serious. "I came to the American Church for two reasons. First, to hear Marcel Dupré, whom I have listened to many times at Notre Dame. Second, because I am searching for something I do not have, something I'm not sure I can even define."

Chapter Two

When Camus asked how I developed my faith, I was startled by his bluntness. I sat back to consider the question. Why did he want to know? His eyes spoke to his sincerity. He did not seem to want to poke holes in my belief system. There was a definite honesty about him, a simple, child-like desire to understand. Still I was unsure how to answer his question. I hadn't discovered my faith at any particular instant or as a result of any event. I grew up in a Christian home where prayer and worship were a part of everyday life. We never ate a meal without my father offering thanks to God for his blessing. My father was not overly pious or saintly, but he lived close to God. My mother, on the other hand, seemed to me to be a living saint. God was an ever-present force in our lives and has continued to act in me.

I finally said, "Through all the experiences of my life, my terrors and my triumphs, God has been present with me. I am convinced that if Jesus meant what he taught— that the Kingdom of God is in the midst of us—then perhaps, God wants all of mankind to build its faith to the point that it can change the world, no matter how many thousands of years it might take to achieve. Faith is far more than the adherence to a set of beliefs or tenets that guide our conduct. Faith is a measure of our whole being and a process that involves a whole lifetime. So rather than begin with faith, perhaps we should begin with the experiences of kindness, respect, helpfulness, and loving concern from which understanding may grow. Once understanding takes root in our being, a righteous, whole-hearted faith develops within us."

Camus listened intently and I began to feel a deepening rapport and trust developing between us. Very slowly and with deep emotion, he began to share with me the story of his childhood. He was raised in Algiers. When Camus was only one, his father died in the Great War. His mother and aunt raised him in abject poverty. His mother was a simple woman, illiterate, and nearly deaf. They lived on the little that she could make working as a charwoman, lacking everything but envying nothing. He eventually won a scholarship to the University of Algiers where he studied Plato, Plotinus, Augustine, Nietzsche, Dostoyevsky, Kierkegaard, and Heidegger. He wrote his Master's thesis on neo-Platonism with an emphasis on Plotinus.

"As a youth," he told me, "I came down with tuberculosis and experienced such pain and anguish that I wanted to die. As an adult, I witnessed the atrocities of Hitler. I saw the burning of the Jews in concentration camps and can testify to the plight of the refugees, milling across the continent, homeless and destitute. I lost all faith in humanity. I realized that I lived in a climate, an age, characterized by violent death and despair. In response, I did two things: I wrote about it, and I joined the Communist Party."

This was not unusual. In Paris, I had found that many people had looked to the Communist Party for some kind of redemption or salvation.

"I thought that the Party's ideals would deliver us from poverty and intolerance. But when I saw Stalin ignore the suffering of his citizens, I could no longer support communism. Many of my friends were able to ignore unethical conduct for the sake of abstract politics, but I could not. I have always been disturbed by the conflict between ideas and their actualities. This is why I am always on the verge of denying that life has any meaning or that the existence of a Supreme Being could bring meaning to this world."

"Can you tell me precisely what caused your disillusionment?" I asked.

Camus leaned forward, resting on one elbow. "For a long time, I believed that the universe itself was a source of meaning, but now I have lost confidence in its rationality."

"Do you mean that we live in an irrational universe?"

"No. I believe that the universe is both rational and irrational. We can make sense of our environment through rational application of science and empirical knowledge, but when it comes to man's most basic questions of meaning and purpose, the universe is silent.

"Ten or twelve years ago, I wrote the *Myth of Sisyphus*. Later I embodied this sense of *ennui* in the fictional character Meursault in my first novel, *The Stranger*. I tried to show that all human attempts to answer the questions of meaning are futile. My basic philosophy is that we human beings have been thrust into existence with neither knowledge of our origin nor help for the future. We have questions about our meaning and purpose that the universe cannot answer. In a word, our very existence is absurd."

"Absurd" was a strange word to use for describing the universe. I knew it was a word he used frequently in his writings, but I was never sure why. "What do you mean by 'absurd'?"

He leaned back in his chair and spread his hands apart before he spoke. "To me, a rational human being's attempt to understand an irrational universe is the definition of absurd. The conflict between human need and the silence of the universe has produced a deep sense of alienation and exile in human beings."

Here he raised an admonitory finger at me, then continued: "The silence of the universe has led me to conclude that the world is without meaning. This silence betokens the evils of war, of poverty, and of the suffering of the innocent. I have been immersed in this suffering and poverty since the rise of Fascism and Hitler's Nazism. So, what do you do? For me, the only response was"—here he pulled one index finger with the other—"to commit suicide, intellectual or physical suicide, or"—here he pulled back his middle finger—"to embrace Nihilism and go on surviving in a world without meaning. All I can do is write about it and keep on writing about it." With that, he went silent.

After a moment, he leaned forward again, and looked past me for a moment before he placed his forehead in the palm of his hand. "Howard," he said, much more slowly and softer than before, "you asked the source of my disillusionment." His eyes lowered again and he stared at the table beneath him, moving his head from side to side. "While I always trusted the universe and humanity in the abstract, my experience made me begin to lose faith in its meaning in practice. Something is dreadfully wrong. I am a disillusioned and exhausted man. I have lost faith, lost hope, ever since the rise of Hitler. Is it any wonder that, at my age, I am looking for something to believe in?" He raised his eyes again until they met mine. "To lose one's life is only a little thing. But, to lose the meaning of life, to see our reasoning disappear, is unbearable. It is impossible to live a life without meaning."

Here he sat before me, head lowered. The depressed look in his eyes was accented by the little pouches of skin under each one. Despite all of his brilliant success and his fame as a writer, sadness remained his dominant emotion. I wondered what he thought as he sat there. How did he think that I, a guest minister from America, could possibly help him? How could I help him find the answers for which he was ardently searching? As I watched him, I realized that his was more than intellectual curiosity. He wanted more than just a comprehension of faith. He wanted to experience this faith and have it act in his own life.

One of the most difficult problems that human beings must face is the existence of evil. It is not a problem exclusive to the religious. Any sensitive person is troubled by the evil and pain in the world. Storms, natural disasters, floods, immorality, lack of concern for others—it seems impossible to reconcile these evils of the world with a benevolent and omnipotent God. At no time was this question harder, at no time these evils more evident, than during and after World War II.

My own experience of the War had been limited. In 1948, I had toured some of Europe and had witnessed the aftereffects of Hitler's atrocities. I had been allowed to tour some of postwar Germany and I had seen many whose lives had been devastated. Men, women, and children had absent limbs and were covered in dirt and surrounded by debris as if the bombs had just fallen. When I returned from Germany to Ohio, I had spent many nights asking the same questions that Camus now raised. Who could blame anyone for questioning the good of God in the wake of such tragedy? Certainly, the question on our minds was the same one that David Hume posed in his *Dialogues Concerning Natural Religion*, "Is God willing to prevent evil and unable? Then he is not omnipotent. Is he able but unwilling? Then he is malevolent. Is he both able and willing? Whence then is evil?"

The inability of countless philosophers to answer these questions has made the problem of evil one of the largest stumbling blocks to the belief in a loving God. (In fact, a whole sub-field of theology addresses this question—theodicy.)

"I honestly believe that the Holocaust was the greatest crime in history. You would have had to have been here then, Howard, to realize the magnitude of the despair and hopelessness that covered us all after the war. It was hard to say why anyone would wish to continue living in such a world. I felt, along with thousands of others, that suicide was the logical conclusion of truth. I believe that this universe, which is capable of killing millions with one bomb, results in a feeling that existence is anguish. I believe that it is a sickness that only death can cure. If there is a God, why does he allow so many innocent people to writhe in anguish?"

"Albert," I said, "I must confess that there are no easy answers. In fact, we are getting into some deep water with this issue. As a minister, I have witnessed many of the difficulties of human existence. I have seen families wiped out by natural disasters, senseless killings, terrible diseases that wrack the body and the mind. I've seen the consequences of sin and selfishness. It may surprise you to know that, faced with the repulsive acts of this world, I have asked myself this same question many times."

We had already been meeting for four hours and could not solve the problem of evil today, so we decide to stop for the time being. As I stepped from the car, he asked, "Do you think we might be able to continue this discussion sometime soon?"

"I should like that very much," I replied. So began a rather unlikely friendship between an American minister from Ohio and a great French Existentialist.

Chapter Three

At the close of our first meeting, Albert and I set a tentative date to get together again, about three weeks later. He was to phone the church office to confirm the appointment. We had no contact during those three weeks, and I began to doubt that he would come for the appointment. I thought our first conversation had gone well, and he had been in church the next two Sundays. I saw him sitting in the back of the sanctuary wearing dark glasses, but both times he left before the end of the service without greeting me at the door. I began to wonder if he was avoiding me. I was working at my desk in my apartment when the secretary rang through. It was one o'clock, and she was calling to inform me that my guest had arrived.

After a few minutes, I entered the reception room.

When Camus saw me enter, he stood up and greeted me warmly. He was dressed immaculately, wearing a dark blue suit despite the July day. He couldn't have been friendlier, and my insecurity in our relationship melted away. We chatted as we walked out the door, but we were quieted as we approached his car.

The American Church is on the *Quai d'Orsay*, which is a very busy street, and they did not allow parking there. When Camus had come in to get me, he had left the car running on the street and ran in to ask the church secretary to call me. Since I had been in the middle of writing some notes and wanted to complete my thought, I was delayed for a minute or two in getting down to the reception room. So when we walked outside, we were surprised to see a police car parked right in front of Camus's car. There were two policemen, one of whom was standing outside of the car waiting for its owner to come out. When we approached, he immediately presented Camus with a ticket for illegal parking. Camus had just stopped to run in and get me, and this was my fault for having dallied.

The policeman asked for Camus' driver's license and they conversed in French. I got into the car to wait, not able to understand what they were saying. Then they stopped talking; the policeman was reading the driver's license for probably the third or fourth time. Then, just like that, the policeman returned the license and tore up the ticket. Then he pulled out a clean sheet of paper for Camus' autograph. Camus signed the sheet and got back into the car. As we started to leave, the second policeman ran up with his sheet of paper and Camus stopped to sign it, too. After we got going, Camus had this look of disgust on his face and said some very uncomplimentary things in French. We drove along the *Quai d'Orsay* beside the Seine with its stone embankments and multitude of trees, and once he had regained his composure, Camus pointed out the small bookstalls that lined the streets and the people walking among them.

After about twenty minutes, we entered the area called Montmartre. It is behind the beautiful, domed *Sacré Cœur* (Church of the Sacred Heart) and is famous for its artist colony where students and professionals gather daily to paint portraits of tourists. After parking the car, Camus donned his customary dark glasses and a wide-brimmed hat. We walked about a block before turning into a side alley and entering a small restaurant. A carved rooster hung above the door; it was *Le Coq*. I would find that this was a favorite place of his. We walked down into the cellar. The headwaiter and Albert Camus greeted each other before we were ushered to a corner table partially hidden behind an old curtained partition. Once seated, Camus removed his glasses and hat. We both ordered red wine, French onion soup, and salad.

As we ate, I said, "Mr. Camus, this is one of the most relaxed days I have had in Paris!"

He looked at me smiling and said, "Will you please call me Albert?" At first I was shocked, but I warmed to the idea when he offered me his hand and we shook on it.

The quiet lunch finished, he reached into his pocket and pulled out several pieces of paper, which he unfolded. "I have here some notes on one of your earlier addresses." He stopped then and corrected himself: "sermons."

The sermon in question was on the Four Great Events

in History. It was one of the first sermons I had delivered in Paris and was based mainly on the Book of Genesis. He named the four great events that I had spoken of: the birth of conscience, the birth of a nation, the birth of a Savior, and the birth of the Church. Then he placed the pages on the table and rubbed his forehead with his fingers.

"After this sermon, I went home and found my Latin Vulgate. I looked up the story of Adam and Eve and the serpent. . . ."

I interrupted him, "Albert, do you not own a Bible in French?"

"No, I have only the Vulgate which my mother and the parish priest gave me as a child."

I was surprised by this. I assumed that a man as well read as he would surely have read the Bible in his native tongue, even if only for its value as literature.

After a moment, he continued his thought, "In your sermon, you talked about Adam and Eve and the tree and the serpent and the flaming sword. You said that we are all actors in a drama and that this drama was the birth of conscience. Howard, would you please tell me how you define 'conscience'?"

I had written the sermon and delivered it originally back home in Ohio, but I was not prepared for that question. What motivated this discussion? The material on Adam and Eve and creation is interesting but why did Camus pick this as an entry point? Was he thinking about the relationship between a God of the universe and the atrocities and evils of Hitler's Nazism? Was he considering the Biblical story of creation and the existence of evil within man's nature?

I fumbled for a moment while I thought. Then I turned the question around, "Well, Albert, what is your understanding of conscience?"

He thought for a moment and then said, "I like the Freudian definition of conscience. In Freudian psychology, conscience is the internalization of the moral lessons given us as children by our parents and teachers."

"That seems to be a pretty good definition of conscience, though I have to think about it for a moment. . . . To me, conscience is an innate feeling of what is right and wrong. It is like moral intuition and usually is accepted without argument. Christian conscience, however, is different. Christian conscience is based on a law, which the person is aware he did not create, but which determines his ethical and moral values. Conscience is an inner voice that guides a person to the love of good and abhorrence of evil, a directive which puts order into a person's social and personal life. To me the birth of conscience caused the change from man-the-animal into man-the-human-being. Before God created conscience, there was nothing within the human animal to which God could appeal.

"The book of Genesis said we were made in the image of God. It presents God as saying, 'Let us make man in our own image; in the image of God he created him.'"

Camus seemed intensely interested when he asked, "But God is not visible, no one has ever seen him, isn't this correct?"

"Certainly the image of God which every human being bears cannot be conceived in physical terms. God is not physical. Jesus said God is a spirit. Men of faith, therefore, have always felt that the image of God is a capacity for spiritual discernment, an awareness between the human soul and God. The Old Testament referred to it as the 'still, small voice,' and Jesus referred to it as 'the light that is in thee.' However we describe it, it is the mark of God upon us."

Camus nodded, "I am following you so far. But let me ask, do you look upon the story of the Garden of Eden as being factual . . . that is, historical?"

This was a big order, and we could have spent the rest of the day discussing nothing else. I said, "When it comes to the historical truth of this story, there are two methods of interpretation. You can think of the story as literal fact—our first ancestor was a man named Adam. Adam succumbed to the temptation offered by his wife. He ate the forbidden fruit, thus committing the original sin. We are all his children and have inherited his guilt. Therefore, we all stand under the condemnation of God.

If you see the story in this way, you think of Adam's fall as having occurred many years ago. If the story is a historical fact, we should hate Adam for getting all of humanity into trouble. We would also hate God for blaming us for what our ancestor did. For me, there is a better way of looking at the story: Adam, in Hebrew, means man. Therefore, what you have here is not a story of what happened to one man, but a dramatization of the way things are with all of us."

Camus was excited by this idea. "Yes, yes, I try to do this in my own writing. It is a mark of all good literature. Adam here is a mirror of human nature."

"That's right. This story is not a piece of ancient history buried in the dead past. It is really a projection of us in the act of being ourselves. Looking into the mirror of Adam, we see that man is a mix of good and evil."

Camus smiled at this. "As Pascal said, 'Man is the glory and the scum of the universe.'"

I liked that and said, "Yes, that is exactly what this story is saying."

With that issue resolved, Albert cut to the chase: "You said something about man being crafted like God?"

"God created man in his own image. In the image of God he created him," I said, reciting the relevant passage. "Man has a capacity for the true, the beautiful, and the good. As such, he differs from every other creature on earth. This capacity is the image of God; it is conscience." I smiled, proud of having finally found my definition.

"But you described God as a man, walking through the garden. If this is not literal, what do you mean?"

"Well, when man cultivates this intimate relationship with God, it is often said that he 'walks with God.' This created world in which we live is the garden through which we walk. In Hebrew, 'Eden' translates as delight, enchantment, or pleasure, but there is another element to this garden, the evil represented by the serpent. Within human nature therefore there is Eden, which is the part made in the image of God, and also this evil, the serpent. In defiance to the will of God, Adam and Eve eat of the forbidden fruit and thereby lose the paradise that God has given them. They are forced to earn their bread by the sweat of their brow, isolated from the delight that is God. The writer of the book of Genesis spoke in pictures, but the meaning is plain enough. Goodness and sin form the double-edged sword of human nature. They devolve into the split personality which we know so well."

"In *Faust*, Goethe wakes up to this fact and cries out, 'Two souls, alas, are lodged within my breast!' So this is what you see when you look in the mirror? You see Adam, part angel, part devil?"

I nodded. "I see a creature made in the image of God, except that we are also possessed of the serpent's fang."

Camus' eyebrows narrowed for a moment. "What is the nature of this serpent, from a religious point of view?"

"The answer is right here in this story. The serpent came to the woman and said to her, 'Did God say that you shall not eat of any tree in the garden?' The woman told him, 'We may eat of the fruit of the trees of the Garden, but God said, "You shall not eat of the fruit of the tree that is in the midst of the garden, neither shall you touch it, lest you die."' But the serpent said to the woman, 'You shall not die, for God knows that when you eat of it, your eyes will be opened, and you will be like God, knowing good and evil.' So the woman took of the fruit and ate. She also gave some to her husband and he ate.

"The story did not say anything about sex, as is often thought. What it did say was that a man and a woman were given a certain command by God, but there was something in their nature which was like the serpent and suggested that God did not know what he was talking about. They succumbed to that suggestion and defied the will of God by asserting their own will over his. In other words, what they did was take God off his throne of power and put themselves in his place, making themselves powerful gods. The issue, Albert, the issue that gnaws at us all is whether God intended for this to happen, and if so, why?"

His reply was, "I once had a typewriter go bad on me. The repairman said that the key in most need of repair was the letter 'I.' He told me that in all of his experiences repairing typewriters, it was this key that needed repair most often. It is not that 'I' is used the most, but that it is hit with a peculiar force."

I chuckled to myself as I sat back and said, "Albert, in light of the Bible, that is the meaning of sin. If you take the word and spell it out—S I N—the middle letter is 'I.' That is the best way of putting the matter that I know. Sin is putting God out of his central place in our lives and putting self in the center. Adam is a picture of human nature, and every new life that enters the world is born with a tendency to do the same thing. You and I cannot get into the world without bringing along a will that attempts to take the place of God. That was the trouble with Adam and Eve. It is the main trouble with most of us. We refuse to give God's place to God; we demand this place for ourselves."

"You're talking about Hitler," Camus replied.

"Absolutely, he was an extreme case, but we are also talking about every human being, and the basis of all evil."

Camus said, "There is a lot of trouble that comes from this, from human beings trying to play God."

I replied, "You are absolutely right. You have written a great deal about the subject of estrangement. You know a lot more about estrangement than I do."

"Yes, but won't you continue. I want to hear what you have to say."

So I continued, "Well, let's take another look at the story. When Adam and Eve heard the sound of God walking in the Garden, do you remember what they did?"

"Yes, I do. They went and hid in the bushes."

I chuckled a bit. "And then what?"

"I don't remember."

"God called to Adam and said, 'Where are you?' and Adam replied, 'I heard the sound of thee in the garden, and I was afraid and hid myself.' God said, 'Have you eaten of the tree which I commanded you not to eat?' And Adam replied, 'The woman whom thou gavest to be with me, she gave me the fruit of the tree and I ate it.' Then God said to the woman, 'What is this that you have done?' The woman said, 'Well, the serpent beguiled me, and I ate.' Therefore the Lord God sent them forth from the Garden of Eden to till the ground from which they sprang. When the man and the woman, who had lived in such happy and intimate fellowship with God, tried to take over and put themselves in his place, they were driven out, cut off, separated and estranged from God."

Suddenly, Camus threw up his arms and said, "Howard, do you remember what Augustine said: 'Thou hast made us for thyself, and our hearts are restless till they find their rest in thee.'?" His face lit up dramatically. Camus was excited by my explanation of man's being cast out from the garden—which related to his own interest in man's estrangement. I said to myself, here is a man who is on the road to becoming a Christian. Here was a key moment, a turning point in this man's life. I could tell by the light in his eyes, the expression on his face, that Camus was experiencing something new in his life.

He said, "That is a great story."

"But it doesn't end there. There's more to it. The trouble does not stop with the estrangement of our selves from

God. Listen to the story: As we all know, two sons were born to Adam and Eve. Their names were Cain and Abel. One day Cain said to his brother, 'Let us go into the field.' When they were in the field, Cain rose up against his brother and killed him. In other words, the sin of putting ourselves in the place where God belongs not only begets estrangement from the divine presence, but causes trouble between other human beings and ourselves. Why did Cain kill Abel? Because he was angry with him. Why was he angry with him? Because he was jealous of him. Because 'The Lord had regard for Abel and his offering, but for Cain and his offering, he had no regard.'

"Cain simply could not stand to see Abel get ahead of him. He could not bear the thought of God having the last word. So he took things into his own hands and killed his brother. Isn't that the source of all family trouble?—Envy, anger, jealousy, rebellion, and selfishness—the demand that I have my way over your way and the refusal to let God have his own way."

Albert stopped to think. There was a long silence before he said, "Howard, if this is true, then when you stop to think about it, it is also the basis for our current race problems."

"You are exactly right. Despite our God being the respecter of persons and in light of the Bible which says that in Christ all human distinctions are wiped out, we still cling to our doctrine of white supremacy, at least in America."

"No, not just in America. This is the same rationale that fueled Nazism—the superiority of the Aryan race. I've seen it in Europe for many, many years. Our sense of omnipotence dies hard. We keep on playing God. Even a blind man can see the estrangement between the larger groups in our nations."

"I recall a wise man saying to a friend, 'The whole trouble in our world is the lack of an apostrophe.' When the friend wanted to know what he meant, he said, 'Well look at Adolph Hitler and at Mussolini and at Josef Stalin and at Hideki Tojo—What you see is this: men trying to be gods instead of trying to be God's.' Yes, sin is rebellion, and rebellion brings war. And this war not only divides men against their Maker, and against other people, but also against themselves."

"Well," Camus said, "It's a great story and I've learned a good deal from it."

"There are a good many more," I said. "I think you would benefit from a modern translation if you are to truly understand Christianity." When our conversation thus ended, I set off immediately to find a French translation of the Bible.

Chapter Four

The very next day, I went to see Dr. Clayton Williams, the Minister of the American Church, and asked him if he had a French translation of the Bible that I could give to a friend.

"I have one," he said, pushing himself up from his desk and walking to the bookshelf. "Anyone in particular?" he asked as he strummed the books with his fingers, finally stopping on one of the bindings and pulling the book from the shelf.

"As a matter of fact, it is for Albert Camus."

Dr. Williams's eyebrows lifted and his forehead crinkled. "Indeed," he said, staring at me over his bifocals. "Well, bring him to my office, and I'll hand him one personally."

I called Camus and asked him to come to the church, so that I could give him something. I greeted him as he arrived that Wednesday and took him upstairs to Dr. Williams's office. Camus took his steps slowly, breathing hard. Until that moment, I did not realize how weak Camus actually was. At the top of the stairs, I helped him to a chair. When he began coughing, I hurried off to get him a glass of water. He had told me that as a youth he had suffered from tuberculosis, but I had not realized how much it had weakened his lungs.

After about ten minutes, we entered Dr. Williams's office. Williams rose from his desk and offered his hand to Camus, saying, "Hello, hello, I am delighted to meet you." Camus took his hand and smiled back. Then Dr. Williams leaned against the front edge of his desk, bracing the book in his lap. He rubbed his hand over the red leather. "It is my pleasure to present you with one modern French translation of the Holy Bible," he smiled, lifting the book until the gold embossed letters faced Camus.

They spoke several sentences in French, and Camus expressed his appreciation before continuing in English for my benefit. "I'm sure that Dr. Mumma will be happy to guide you in learning to read the Bible. I hope you will find some wisdom in it." He said this with a smile as he studied Camus and his reaction.

"Of that I am sure," Camus said, and there was a brief lull. "Well, I'm afraid I can't stay long," he said. At that, I walked Camus back down to his car. He thanked me again before climbing back into his car and pulling away with the Bible in the seat beside him.

I did not see Camus for some time. He stopped attending church, and I wondered why. Then one evening, I was sitting beside the window in my living room watching couple after couple strolling beside the Seine, when the secretary's buzzer called me to the phone. "Howard," Albert said energetically, "I have finished the books of Genesis and Exodus and was very excited by the stories of the journey of the children of Israel to the Promised Land."

My spirit revived when I heard his voice. "That's wonderful," I said. "I am glad you are enjoying them."

"But," he continued, with notably less enthusiasm, "I am now on the book of Numbers, having skipped over much of Leviticus. In fact, I find these two books very boring." He made another sound as if clearing his throat, before he continued, "I would like to speak to you about what I have read."

I laughed a bit and said, "Albert, even though the Bible is literature, you don't have to read it as if it were a novel or a play."

Some days later, we again drove to *Café Le Coq* in Montmartre. We sat at the same table, assisted by the same waiter, and again enjoyed red wine and delicious onion soup. Camus started right in, "I did enjoy the stories I read, and I liked the teachings very much. But, I would like to ask you one important question—do you take everything in the Bible seriously?"

"The Bible is not a work of science"—I was prepared for this question. "It is no longer possible to accept as literal truth every statement the Bible makes. Without doubt, numbers of historical mistakes have been discovered. The Bible from time to time also runs counter to the mass of our scientific knowledge. Still, it is wrong to argue that because of some mistakes, the entire Bible should be ignored. None of the writings of even the greatest historians and scientists is entirely free of error, but we do not discard the whole of their works. We simply go on applying the usual tests of truth."

"I am hearing something new here, and I like this line of reasoning." Albert said, with his hands clasped before him.

This sounded like a good beginning, so I continued. "Much of the evidence about God and his Son, Jesus, and about the Spirit of God has been discussed down through the centuries by the Christian church. Most of the evidence about these subjects comes from the Bible. On the other hand, the Bible is concerned with a reality beyond the scope of science and history. There are some thinkers who dismiss the Bible as simply a collection of fables with no basis in fact or relevance in our lives. The world could not have been made in six days. Jonah could not have been swallowed by a great fish. Jesus could not have physically risen from the dead. For these reasons, many dismiss the entire Bible as incredible.

"These people fail to distinguish between two different types of truth. The first form, factual truth, is found in statements that can be described, heard, and televised. The second form, parable or truth conveyed by story, is something that does not claim to be factually true but is nevertheless intended to express a basic truth—about God, the world, or man and the human condition. For example, there are many statements in Genesis that stretch credulity. These have to be checked very carefully.

But, as we discussed with the story of Adam and Eve, Genesis can also tell us something about human nature—there is good and evil in all of us."

"This is what I strive for in my stories," Camus said, nodding. "The objective is to illuminate some higher truth, even if the story itself is a fiction."

"Yes," I said, "and more than that, the basic truths are more likely to be understood by ordinary people if they are told in the form of a story. Could you have more succinctly captured the French people's feelings of estrangement than you did with *The Myth of Sisyphus*? In the same way, the early chapters of Genesis, the book of Jonah, the narratives of the death and physical ascension of Jesus are examples of the second form of truth. This is not to say that they are untrue. They tell us some very true things about human life and the universe in which we live.

"I have often thought of these stories as a drama in four acts. In Act I, we find God's choice of Abraham to be the founder of the nation, Israel, through which God could save the world. We also see the early history of this nation until it escapes from Egypt. Then in Act II, we see the wanderings of the new nation. We are told of their settlement in Canaan and their rise to power. We hear the prophets attempt to recall Israel to its true destiny. We witness the prophets' failure and the defeat of Israel and eventually the exile of the two sections of the nation.

"In Act III, we learn how God brings back one part of his nation from exile and establishes this smaller nation to be his agent. Thus, the hope of God's true salvation is kept alive. Lastly, in Act IV, Jesus comes to preach and establish God's rule. He is opposed and killed, but he defeats evil and death and sends his apostles out to the ends of the earth. We even have an epilogue, which is mainly found in the book of Revelation. It describes the final battle between good and evil and the victory of God through Jesus Christ.

"The New Testament takes for granted, and doesn't trouble to repeat, the Old Testament. Yet the meaning of the Old Testament is only to be seen when it is brought to fruition in the New Testament. The Bible, as a whole, shows that God has been giving to and taking from man for as long as man has walked the earth, through all of history. This give and take is what the Bible sets out to describe. For the Christian, the climax of this interaction comes with the birth of Jesus the Christ, the Messiah. To appeal to the emotional nature of man, the entire scheme is set out in the form of a historical drama.

"If the Bible is viewed in this way, despite the fact that it is composed of separate books and chapters, everything starts to fall into place. Many puzzling, even contradictory passages begin to make sense, as long as one remembers that the Bible is a collection of works compiled over a thousand or more years. It is not surprising, given the time span, that this collection lacks perfect order, or that the authors do not all share the same point of view."

Camus frowned, "I have noticed this in my readings of the Bible, that some of the stories are told over and over again and there are many inconsistencies. . . ."

"The most remarkable thing about the Bible is not that there are so many differences and inconsistencies, but that it has survived the lack of a solid, unwavering consensus among its authors. Thus the Bible gives a reliable but not

infallible record of the character of God and his relations
with the human race and all of its members. I believe that
all of its authors were inspired by the Spirit of God in such
a way that their own abilities and powers were not sus-
pended or abolished but rather enhanced and developed in
cooperation between their minds and spirits and the Spirit
of God. In the end we can call the Bible the word, but not
the words, of God."

Camus nodded, but did not say anything. Apparently
he was unsure of where to go next.

"I remember Bishop John Robinson's book *Can We
Trust the New Testament?* Trust is a good word to use.
When we trust people, we recognize their jokes as jokes,
their metaphors as metaphors, and their fishing stories as
the tall tales that they are, but we also recognize that on
important matters they do not lead us astray. It is the same
way with the Bible. Despite the qualifications we have
noted, it won't lead us fundamentally astray. It remains the
ultimate guide to Christian faith and life.

"So, is the Bible true? Can it be trusted? Is it faithful to
life? The Hebrew word that we translate as truth carries
the connotation of trustworthiness or steadfastness or
faithfulness much more than the connotation of precise
historical fact. The true person in Hebrew is the one that
you can trust. It is the same for the Bible."

Camus interrupted, "I once read or heard that the Bible
is regarded as the Word of God, but I do not understand
what this means."

"It is called the Word of God because it is primarily a
record of God's revelation as well as the evolution of the
faith of the ancient Israelites. The Israelites were an extra-

ordinary people who possessed a genius not only for religion but also for morality. Their leaders were passionately
concerned with human conduct. They wanted to ensure
that conduct was brought into conformity with God's
word not only individually but also nationally. They
believed that people must adjust their actions to fit moral
law.

"It is reasonable that God gave the world a revelation
of himself—the Bible as the Word of God. Part of our
shared faith is that God still makes use of the Bible to display his righteousness and the availability of his love,
mercy, and forgiveness. Reading the Bible, you may find
yourself confronted by God and thinking about God. The
Bible presents a philosophy of history that throws light on
problems faced by human beings through all ages. The
Psalms and the Prophets still speak to us today—the teachings of Jesus remain as a living voice. I have found that
words, written long ago by a prophet or psalmist, may
suddenly become God's personal message to me, more
than two thousand years later. A passage may expose a
hidden sin and call us to repentance, or quiet a lingering
fear, or bring courage and comfort in a time of trial."

After a period of quiet and thought, Camus raised a
profound issue. "Tell me, Howard, does the Bible throw
light on present-day world problems?"

After a moment of thought, I replied, "There are no easy
answers to that question. The guiding principles of life for
me are contained in Bible lessons. 'They that take up the
sword shall perish by the sword.'" I paused to see if Camus
followed my thoughts. "'We are members one of another. If
one member suffers, all the members suffer with him.' I

believe this clearly says that we, as nations, should not engage in economic and financial acts that are to the disadvantage of other people, even if we are to gain from them."

"How true that is," Camus agreed.

"'God has made the world and all things therein and has made of one blood all the nations of men for to dwell on the face of the earth.'—We must act the same toward all men regardless of our differences."

Camus nodded.

"'Seek ye first the Kingdom of God and its righteousness and all things shall be added unto you.' . . . Woe unto you if you do not seek first the general welfare but instead seek individual gain and national advantage."

Camus chuckled and nodded again.

"Here God speaks directly to the economic chaos, the mass unemployment, and the conflict between classes of the last hundred years. He gives us the key to the understanding of the universe and names the work we have to do to bring the Kingdom of God to us. His power works for our redemption. It convinces us that we are not alone.

"With these confusions out of the way, it is easier to see what the Bible really is. It is a library of very different books. It contains histories, poems, hymns, letters, and the four Gospels. But, all these books have the same purpose: to set out with the greatest possible force a particular view of God and the world and mankind. The subject is God, the world, and everything it contains. The history, literature, and teachings on conduct are all subordinate to this."

"I have enjoyed my readings very much, and it seems I read them very much as you did, as stories that tell us something about life."

"That is good, but you have not truly read the Bible yet." Camus looked troubled by this statement, the brows over his eyes furrowed. "You still read the Bible through the eyes of a scholar or literary critic, not as a Christian would. You cannot probe the Bible in depth until you look beyond the scholarship."

Camus seemed confused, as if fighting to understand my words. But finally he said, "I will continue to try."

Chapter Five

One evening while dining with Jacques and his family, I mentioned that on the next Wednesday I was going to have lunch with a French celebrity, Albert Camus. Right away the concierge's wife said to me, "Oh, Dr. Mumma, won't you let Nicolette and me prepare a lunch for you and Mr. Camus? We could serve it in your apartment living room. We would love to do that!"

"That would be fine. I would be glad to pay you," I responded.

"Oh, meeting him would be payment enough."

"No, if you want to prepare a light lunch for us, I will pay for the food. That is the only way that you can do it." Finally, they agreed.

My appointment with Albert had already been scheduled. When the time for our visit arrived I waited downstairs, not wanting a repeat of our previous performance with the police. When I saw his car pull up in front of the church, I met him at the curb. I told him that we had been invited to have lunch with the concierge and his family in my apartment. For a moment he looked distraught, he looked away, as if considering the idea. He was almost a shy man at times, very protective of his private life. He took every opportunity to avoid unwanted exposure. He often went to great lengths to reserve tables in some hidden corner of a restaurant where we wouldn't be disturbed or even seen. But after only a moment of thought, he turned back to me and smiled, thanking me for the invitation.

This was the first time he had been in my apartment. The table was all set, and Jacques' wife and daughter, Suzanne and Nicolette, were ready to pour iced tea and bring in fruit salad. It was quite a production! They had gone to great lengths to get everything prepared for us and were very polite, pausing only to smile as they served, or to ask Camus if he wanted anything more. Lastly, they left us alone as soon as the meal was finished so that we could have some privacy, a gesture that Camus seemed to appreciate. It occurred to me, watching how differently people acted in his presence, that it could not be easy for him, a private man trying to avoid the public eye.

"Tell me, Albert, did you have any interest in Christianity before we met? It's not something that many people would expect from you. . . ."

Camus laughed. We were sitting in front of a large living room window that overlooked the street and, of course, the Seine. He watched the people walking past as he replied, "No, there are many things about me that people would not expect." He thought some more. It was an overcast day, but the clouds cleared just enough to let some sun through as he continued. "Let me tell you about a friend, Simone Weil. As a philosophical theologian, you would have enjoyed knowing her."

"I would love to have a chance to meet her."

Camus shook his head slowly: "She died some years ago, in 1943, at the age of thirty-four."

"I'm sorry," I said. Camus just gave a half-hearted shrug to show that he was not bothered. I asked, "How did you meet her?"

"She sent me a letter in 1939, asking me to clarify something I had written." He scratched the side of his face with his fingers, squinting slightly. "I can't recall exactly what it was, but she wrote again several weeks later asking for an audience. After several polite refusals, I finally succumbed and invited her to tea at my apartment." He laughed again, smiling as he remembered her first visit. "I did not know what to expect. I was wholly taken aback when the maid ushered in this young, weird-looking woman wearing a large-brimmed, black hat and a black dress to match. She was of medium height and not very healthy looking. I must admit, I never before had seen a French woman so plainly dressed and unimpressive looking. I had to wonder what I had let myself in for that afternoon!

"But this woman, so unimpressive in appearance, would turn out to be one of the most intelligent, best educated, original thinkers and social activists that I have ever encountered." Camus went on to list off her accomplishments: "She was one of the first women ever to earn entrance to the *Ecole Normale Supérieure*, receiving a baccalaureate with honors at fifteen. When she graduated in 1931, at twenty-two, she was seventh in a class of 107 and qualified as a teacher of philosophy. She willingly gave up her advantages in order to identify with the poor and suffering. She nearly starved herself to death, and suffered some twelve years of bad health as a result.

"During her brief teaching career, she spent interim periods of hard, practical, and idealistic work as a factory worker and rural laborer. During the Civil War, she voluntarily lived on the wages of and shared the life of the worst paid workers in Spain. And, somehow, she still managed to write reams of essays on such learned subjects as 'A New Renaissance,' 'Rootedness, Culture, and Value,' 'Rights, Justice, and Love,' and 'The Non-Necessity of God.' She came to inspire an enviable host of admirers including T. S. Eliot, Malcolm Muggeridge, and Russell Kirk, all of whom paid highest tribute to her.

"We became friends, and, over a period of several years, we discussed a wide range of topics. We met every few weeks. She would often read an essay that she had written, and then we would spend an hour or so discussing it. We discussed the place of labor in society and the condition of workers, not only in France, but throughout Europe. Simone had a deep conviction that the concept of work in our society needed to be revitalized—just as Gandhi and Marx had done in theirs. Labor needed to be tied to an understanding of work that was spiritual. She was relentless in her belief that civilization could be bettered, and she believed that she had an important message to those who were struggling with work's meaning.

"She maintained a steady interest in work as a central feature of culture throughout her intellectual life. Several of her essays talked of human personality, in which she described the true basis of what it means to be human. She was also concerned with the role of science in modern life and what it had become. She was one of the first writers to point out that while technology in itself is good, it can be used for evil purposes, for example, environmental degradation. She believed that, with the emergence of a full-blown technological society, the problems that accompany technology had grown more apparent and more menacing. She argued that, in the modern period, science was ironically laying the groundwork for an increasingly irrational and unintelligible world. In such a world, human beings would find it more difficult to act in a reasonable or ethical way. She maintained that the essential relationship between labor and thought in human life was being destroyed by modern science. In the process so was human liberty. By 1939, she had increasingly turned to theology and spirituality.

"Of all the subjects that Simone and I discussed, the conversations that most influenced me were those of her religious odyssey. Her quest was to find how and where God's goodness and love could be mediated to humanity outside historical, or more accurately, institutional Christianity. She identified four basic categories for the love of God: the love of neighbors, the beauty of the world, religious practices, and friendship. These forms of love bore the mark of God's power to lift the human being into the very presence of the unknown."

"How did this woman, at such an early age, come to believe in God through the study of philosophy?"

"She was raised in a well-educated, secular, Jewish family and, as a child, never took religion seriously. She didn't think much about God, neither affirming nor denying his existence. Even when she was ill or depressed, it never occurred to her that she might seek divine intervention through prayer. She was brought up to believe that in life every individual was basically on his own. Your ideas about life, your moral values and concepts of right and wrong, were mainly shaped by the conventions of the community in which you were raised. In order to live life well, you develop skills through your education. These skills help you develop excellence in life.

"To develop these necessary skills, Simone was sent to college. In the *Ecole Normale Supérieure,* she began to read Greek philosophy. For the first time in her young life, she heard that there was something more to the universe than the natural world in which we live. She was introduced to an entirely new set of ideas. Plato's dialogues, "Phaedo," "Laws," and "Republic" taught her about transcendent essences. Something in this world is good or true or beautiful because that something participates in a larger, transcending essence that can be directly experienced. The good, the true, and the beautiful are united in a supreme creative principle that can evoke moral affirmation and emotional response within an individual.

"About this time, Simone began to take the reality of her own inner life seriously. Her studies brought a new awareness of the significance of her inner being. She experienced an awakening consciousness of her moral and intellectual character. For the first time, she felt a need for commitment to something outside of herself. This desire for something more was reinforced by reading Plato. He taught her that the human mind was something special and that, through the development of intellect and will, one might attain union with a divine principle or idea in the Platonic sense. Education for her ceased to be about the development of secular skills and became a service of her inner being. Indeed, education would become the means through which her intellect might experience a direct encounter with eternal ideas and the transcendent intelligence that rules and orders the universe.

"Her studies excited her. She began to believe in a world ruled not by blind chance or materialistic mechanics but by a 'wondrous regulating intelligence.' She also came to know that this intelligence was reflected in the human mind and that the mind is capable of knowing something of this wondrous intelligence. Aristotle took her further by teaching her that there is something more in the developing mind than that which comes from sensory experience. The embryonic mind receives a 'seed that comes in from outside'—an eternally active, divine seed. This divine intellect, of which everyone has a potential share, is immortal and transcendent. This intellect is what distinguishes humans from other animals. This active intellect alone gives the human mind the capacity to grasp final and universal truth. It is through this power of human thought that one may comprehend eternal truth, and a human being's highest happiness exists in the contemplation of eternal truth.

"Lastly, Aristotle taught her that, to account for the universe's order and movement, there must be a Supreme

Form, an already existing actuality—eternal and absolute in its perfection. This Supreme Form is the first cause of the Universe and is characterized by the activity of thought. God is, therefore, pure mind. In absolute perfection, God moves by drawing all creation toward himself. God is the goal of all the universe's aspirations and movements. God is the ultimate goal of all human beings. Every individual can try to imitate the Supreme Being, striving to fulfill his own purpose, to grow, mature, and achieve his realized form. God 'moves as the object of desire.' God is hidden, far removed from this world. There is a considerable distance between the human being and God, yet, because the human's highest faculty—his intellect—is divine, he can, by cultivating that intellect and thereby imitating the Supreme Being, bring himself into communion with the Transcendent.

"From this, Simone began to affirm that she could be inwardly grasped by the Transcendent. The result was an intense emotional response and a mystical rapture, an 'over of wisdom.' She began to be grasped, intellectually and emotionally, and was drawn into a commitment to the Transcendent.

"It was out of this concept of the Transcendent that she experienced love for all people with whom she met. She began to see that when we love our neighbor, we are truly loving God. It was this deep conviction that led to her identify herself with the poor and the socially inferior." He smiled at that and sat back in his chair. "She worked for the French Resistance, too, but she eventually starved herself to death, refusing to eat while the victims of the war still suffered."

He turned again to look out the window and took a few moments to think before continuing: "She will be remembered as a warmhearted, generous human being whose writings will, someday, move mountains for many readers."

I could see why this woman had such an effect on him. "It sounds like her understanding of God went beyond the merely philosophical," I said.

Camus smiled, "Yes. I wish I could find whatever it was that moved her thinking." He paused and, turning back toward me, he said, "You know, I have made a great deal of money because I have been somehow able to articulate man's disillusionment in man. I have written things that have meant a great deal to many people. You've seen how they treat me, Howard. I touched something in them because they identified in my writings the anguish and despair that they all felt. I spoke to the meaninglessness and uncertainty, the basic tenets of which I am uncertain I still believe. This, more than anything, is what distresses me, this is the root of my despair."

His eyes looked sleepy and the muscles in his face seemed to relax. He clasped his hands together and pressed them against his lips, staring off somewhere else. I could do nothing but watch—watch and despair with him.

Chapter 6

It was an unusually warm evening in Paris; I was sitting in the living room of my apartment at the American Church. The windows were open, and I was in front of them in a rocking chair. My mind was preoccupied with the exciting events of the past few days. I was startled to hear the buzzer ring. Jacques was on the phone. He said that I had a visitor in the waiting room—"Mr. Albert Camus would like to see you." Because of the late hour, I was surprised, but I asked Jacques to bring him up and to please use the lift. I met them in the hallway. I ushered Camus into the apartment and offered him a chair. He was, surprisingly, dressed for the warm evening. He wore dark trousers with an open-collared, short-sleeved, white shirt. Even though it was late, he seemed very much awake. He smiled and apologized for the hour, saying that as he drove past he saw the lights on and thought he would stop in for a brief visit.

Every afternoon Suzanne, Jacques's wife, brought fresh jars of lemonade and tea up to my refrigerator. So, I poured Albert a glass of tea and immediately told him that I had met a friend of his.

He asked, "And who was that?"

Before I answered his question, I had to set the stage, "Arthur Limorise, assistant and business manager for the Church, and I often start out on walks in the late afternoon. We visit the Luxembourg Gardens, the art galleries, or the antique shops along the *Boulevard Saint-Germain*. Yesterday, after one of our walks, we stopped at a sidewalk café on the *Boulevard Parnasse*. We were seated and had just ordered our dinner, when Arthur tapped me on the arm to point out a couple that sat three tables away. The man was short, black haired, and his eyes were unusual— we would say he was wall-eyed. He seemed quite nervous.

"Arthur asked, 'Do you know who that is?' I had to admit that I did not, so he told me, 'That is Jean-Paul Sartre; his companion,' an attractive young woman, 'is Simone de Beauvoir.'"

Camus seemed amused by this, "Really? You must tell me about it."

So I did. "When we were about halfway through dinner, five university-age students approached Sartre's table and pulled up chairs. A few minutes later, another five or six young people came along. They started to converse with Sartre. From what Arthur told me, this ritual takes place three or four evenings a week. Sartre seemed very much at ease with these young people. He was comfortable chatting with these students who were 20 and 30 years his junior. For the most part, they were all entranced by his explanations of his thinking.

"As I looked at the faces of those young, postwar, university students, I failed to see one face that revealed any sort of happiness. They seemed to be painfully aware that life was not a very meaningful experience. The young people wore the clothing that seems to be the uniform of existentialists and intellectuals—black suits, white shirts, and narrow, dark ties. They seemed to be searching for something to believe in, something that they hoped that Sartre could teach them. Some of them talked, and he conversed with them freely. Others were quiet and introverted, only listening. They shared with him the feelings of loneliness and alienation that his philosophy seemed to touch in them.

"Sartre talked to them until very late, and soon there were so many students that they started spilling around our table until we became a part of the group. I took the opportunity to jot down some notes while he talked. For the most part, Sartre seemed to want to be sure that everyone understood precisely what existentialism was. He talked about the roots of existentialism and said that man creates truth. He said this in familiar words—'There is no god except man, no source above man but the ideas that he discovers and the values that he adopts.'

"A second idea Sartre told the young people was that man is fundamentally a miserable being. The reason he is miserable is that there is no god. It surprised me that Sartre thought it was a horrible thing that there is no god. He said that 'man is painfully aware that he is a free, spiritual being who must determine his own way. There is no help from any outside source. Man is therefore born to be a creature of anguish and forlornness precisely because he is a creature of responsibility. He stands or falls by the virtue or vice of the values he invents and the choices he makes.'

"Again and again, he stressed that man is horribly alone. Man can not even be identified with nature, for nature is ruled by necessity. Sartre emphasized that man is not ruled by biology but by principles that he has created and the uncoerced choices he has made. Man is a moral or spiritual creature who can trace his freedom to neither biology nor God. Man knows nothing of his origin; he simply exists and only with his existence as a free being can thought begin.

"The idea that Sartre expressed that most impressed me was that of involvement. He emphasized that man must risk something. He must become entangled in the experience of fellow men and assist them in the pursuit of freedom. This idea, that man can not remain aloof from risk, is something that I very much agree with. He is to be involved at any cost in the suffering and sacrifice of others. He must accept the common anguish and forlornness of humanity in order to attain the freedom that is man's highest good. The young people seemed to drink in every word Sartre spoke. They seemed to lighten up a bit and feel that they had a goal, a mission in life, and Sartre was somehow the guide to that goal.

"The meeting broke up shortly after midnight and, to my surprise, Arthur walked over and introduced himself to Sartre. They chatted for a while before Arthur came back and said, 'Sartre is willing to meet with you.' He escorted me to their table and introduced me to Sartre and his companion, Simone.

"Surprisingly enough, Sartre asked, 'Would you like to meet some time tomorrow?' I quickly agreed and we made arrangements to meet the next day at his apartment around eleven o'clock."

Camus had been listening intently, but I asked, "Are you bored? Shall I go on?"

"By all means," he said, "I am interested for reasons I will share with you later."

So, I continued, "For three or four hours that night, I contemplated what I would ask him. Eventually I drew up four basic questions by lamplight.

"At the appointed time, Arthur and I approached the second floor apartment and, admittedly, I was a bit nervous in anticipation of meeting our host. The door opened and we were graciously admitted by Simone de Beauvoir. She said she was glad to see us, as Sartre entered from the kitchen with a tray of glasses filled with wine. I was a bit surprised by the condition of the apartment. It was very clean and only sparsely furnished. The carpeting on the floor was well worn and the furniture—table, chairs, and radio—was quite old. There was a Tiffany chandelier with red, white, and amber pieces of glass that seemed out of place—it did not look very French.

"The three of us sat at the table and immediately had a glass of wine. Simone de Beauvoir, who I don't think had said ten words on the previous night, sat apart, over in a corner. She didn't write, she just sat and listened. We were offered two or three different types of wine and open-faced egg or chicken salad sandwiches. There were some nectars and a little tea as well.

"'So, tell me a little bit about your church,' Sartre said, as we began to eat. I told him about the American Church in Paris, which he admitted he had never heard of. Then he wanted to know about me.

"'You and I are fairly close in age,' he said, 'but despite the fact that I am only four years older, it seems our childhoods were very different.' I was born in a happy home; he admitted, quite frankly, that he was born into a very unhappy one. When he was only a year old, his father died. His mother remarried soon afterward, and the marriage turned out to be catastrophic. His maternal grandparents were apparently quite good to him, but his childhood was still miserable. Throughout his early school life, he felt lonely and alienated. He was taunted and called 'the wall-eyed boy' as a result of his cross-sightedness. But by the time he graduated from the *Ecole Normale Supérieure,* he had begun to find himself.

"'Once that happened,' he said, 'the taunting ended. It was as if my tormentors lost themselves just when I found myself.' He paused for a moment, considering his last statement before he continued. 'One of the most powerful influences on me was my experience with the war—both during my service in the army and the time I spent in a German prisoner-of-war camp. It was in the camp that I realized that living in a sense of detachment was not possible in a world dominated by war, torture, and genocide. After I was liberated from the prison camp, I decided that literature would be my commitment. With that vehicle, I would develop a complete philosophy of life that would include morality and man's realization that he is free and is therefore responsible for his own actions.'

"Right away I could see that Sartre was a man of extreme confidence. I got the feeling that I had come to a lecture rather than a discussion, so I asked, 'Have you ever read Kierkegaard?'

"'Yes, I read some of his works, but I did not care for them. Mostly, I have been influenced by Nietzsche's stress on human freedom, the same with Dostoyevsky—despite the latter's being rooted in the context of a specific belief in a moral god and personal immortality, which I cannot accept.' Finally, he said, 'Tell me, Howard, is there anything from the discussion last night that you might wish to pursue this afternoon?'

"'Yes, as a matter of fact, there is,' I said, opening the sheet of paper I had prepared. 'In view of your emphasis upon the freedom or spirituality of the human personality, why do you leave unanswered the question of man's non-material origin?' I reminded him that several times in the evening with the students he used the expression 'man is thrust into the anguish of freedom' as though he had been thrust by someone or something.

"'I must admit that I frequently use that expression. However, I refuse to consider further the question of origin' —he was completely unshaken by the question. 'I have no answers to this question, but I emphatically deny any natural or biological origin for the spiritual freedom with which man is cursed or blessed, as you may see it. Now let us move to the present fact of man's painful freedom.'

"I decided to push him a little further on this point and said, 'This is sort of a metaphysical tour de force. The question cannot be left unanswered by the soul. Can you offer some kind of answer to this question?'

"He seemed somewhat annoyed by my pressing him, and said, 'There is no source of man's spirituality. Man is a spiritual being, but the origin of the spirit is not within himself nor is it in any outside source. Now, let us drop this subject and proceed to the present fact of man's painful freedom—a far more relevant and timely subject.'

'But if there is no God, and if nature has not produced man's freedom, are you saying that man's freedom has produced itself and that man is, perhaps through evolution, his own creator?' I refused to be sidetracked.

"I have never given much thought to that question and am unable to answer it. But, what man does with his freedom is of undisputed importance.'

"As Sartre refused to answer my question, I had to relinquish it, but I was still curious. What man does with the anguish and glory of his freedom is important, but to me the origin of that freedom may determine its nature and use. 'From purely a pragmatic point of view, the source of our freedom cannot be ignored.'

"Sartre agreed, looking a little defeated. 'I would prefer to discuss more timely subjects, but as you wish—what is the explanation of the Christian point of view?'

"'Well, I have to agree with you that, on the subject of freedom, the Christian answer does not exempt man from existence or from the anguish and responsibility that existence provides. Indeed, Christianity requires responsibility. The great difference is that your philosophy is attached to a meaningless world. Christianity's answer comes partly from reason and partly from reason transcended, that is, from revelation. Reason demands that from nothing, nothing may come. Hence man, who finds himself free, could not have created his own freedom. He cannot be his own creator. Nature might be the mother but could not be the father of man's spirituality. Only one possibility remains on rational grounds, namely that a power and an intelligence capable of producing man's freedom must have created man.

"'Revelation moves beyond these arguments of reason to declare that God exists, that he is the rewarder of those who diligently seek him, that he has made us and not we ourselves. He moved of his own redemptive volition out of pure spirit into history, supremely in the form of Jesus Christ. The answer of revelation requires the response of intuition and faith in addition to the assent of reason. Yet, if men of moral earnestness truly behold Jesus Christ, it is not reason alone but direct apprehension that rises within them to declare that Christ is not only the Son of Man, as he called himself, but also the Son of God. Christ himself said to Peter, 'Flesh and blood had not revealed this unto thee, but my father which is in heaven.'

"'The Christian answer, while requiring both existence and responsibility, tells man the news that is almost too good to be true: Mankind is not alone. Christianity and your philosophy both require responsibility and freedom. To you, responsibility is the structure of the universe, the character of power and process and purpose—the very nature of God.'

"'This is a very interesting comparison,' Sartre admitted, 'I have not heard this reasoning before and will have to think on it further.'

"Concerned that he may be tiring of the conversation, I asked if he wished to continue. 'Why, we could spend days doing this. I love it. But I can see you have another question.'

"'Yes, of course,' I said. My second question grew out of the previous night's discussion and was another form of the first: 'Is the world meaningful or meaningless?'

"Sartre took no time to think about it: 'The only meaning that exists, man has created. Man has found no purpose in life except to refuse slavery and pursue freedom.'

"My reaction to his answer was that if God does not exist, man is man's god and is the sole creator to whom tribute must be given. 'It seems to me that the man who will not have God worships himself as a god—a tribute which presupposes the creating of the intelligence that was created.'

"Sartre was silent, so I followed with what I felt was my most important question: 'What, therefore, should be regarded as the nature of morality? Shall the basis of action be absolute morality coming to man from above to influence his nature, or expedience that is enlightened by self-interest?'

"He replied immediately, 'The sole basis of ethics is the fact of freedom.' He said it again with more emphasis the second time: 'The sole basis of ethics is the fact of freedom. Therefore, whatever assists the growth of freedom is moral and whatever hinders the growth of freedom is immoral.' 'Freedom,' I have come to learn, is the key word to understanding Sartre.

"This, of course, is the only ethical principle that could be based on Sartre's philosophy. As he talked, I could not help feeling he had torn an important page from the book of Christ. In Christianity, the requirements of freedom in soul and society are the basis of morality. The difference is that, in Christianity, man pursues the requirements of freedom in the presence of a moral absolute, a holy good.

"But, as Sartre explained it, man pursues freedom witnessed only by himself. The 'self' in whose presence man pursues freedom is self prior to good and independent of moral demand. That is to say, when Sartre spoke of ethics, he spoke of the ethics of strict accountability based on individual responsibility. He said, 'If man is what he makes of himself, then he has no one, except himself, to blame for what he is. Moreover, in the process of choosing for himself, he is choosing not only for himself, but also for all men. He is, therefore, responsible not only for himself, but for all men. Before a man can choose a path of action for himself, he should first ask what would happen if everyone else acted so. This makes his mode of action relevant to all people.'

"Sartre seemed to be calling attention to one of the clearest experiences of human beings: 'All men must choose and make decisions. Although they have no authoritative guide, they must still choose and at the same time ask if they would be willing for others to choose the same action. The act of choice, then, is one that all men must make with a deep sense of anguish—'anguish' was another key word for Sartre—'for in this one act men are responsible not only for themselves but for each other.' 'The Golden Rule,' I said in recognition.

"He simply shrugged and said, 'I do not wish to invoke any universal law to guide man's choice. I am doomed to have no other law than my own.' He paused for a moment before he began again, 'Even though we create our own

values and therefore create ourselves, we nevertheless create, at the same time, an image of our human nature which
is our essence as we believe it should be. When we choose
this or that way of acting, we affirm the value of what we
have chosen. Nothing can be better for any one of us
unless it is better for all of us.'

'That sounds a bit like Kant's categorical imperative,' I
said. Sartre frowned at me when I said that, but made no
comment for a while, leaving me to wonder whether he
was frowning at my conclusion or my reference to Kant, or
both.

"I asked my fourth question: 'What, then, is the chief
end of man?'

"The answer was already obvious: 'The pursuit of freedom.' He paused, and then added, 'Volumes could be written classifying the various kinds of freedom that we pursue: adultery, murder, the Holocaust, and genocide in general. All these principles of conduct have been created by
man in pursuit of freedom. They are, therefore, in terms of
expedience, related to morality.'

"Sartre accepted Nietzsche's dictum, 'God is dead.' But
he also accepted Dostoyevsky's statement, 'If God did not
exist, everything would be permitted.' In a godless world,
man's condition is one of abandonment—a conclusion that
Sartre got from Heidegger. By abandonment, he meant
that the dismissal of God also eliminates every possibility
of finding values in some sort of intelligible heaven. 'Man's
abandonment is a consequence of the fact that everything
is indeed permitted. Therefore, man is forlorn because he
cannot find anything to rely upon within or outside himself. Man is without excuse. His existence precedes his

essence. Apart from his existence there is nothingness. There is only the present.'

"'Were you reared as an atheist, a Protestant, or a Roman Catholic?' I asked. 'And has any particular event in your life particularly influenced your thought?'

"Sartre said his background was nominally Roman Catholic. Then he said, 'France is nominally Roman Catholic, but in reality it is pagan.' He thought some more, then said, 'As I told you earlier, the one particular event that most influenced me was my year in a German prisoner-of-war camp. I discovered firsthand some of the horrible forms of slavery that man's freedom has created. There I also discovered the stage. My first plays were written for the prison theater.'

"As we came to the end of our discussion, I noticed that Simone was still sitting in her chair, listening. She hadn't spoken the entire time. I only had one last question I wanted to ask: 'Do you believe in love?'

"'Yes, I believe in love,' Sartre said, 'but there is no love apart from the deeds of love.'

"'You and I agree on the power of love and that love should result in actions. But I, as a Christian, believe not only in love, but also in a divine lover of men's souls.'

"As we came away and said our good-byes to Sartre and Simone, I could not help thinking Sartre was a man of great ability and vitality. He might even move in the direction of the Christian faith, compelled to do so by the very necessities of the freedom he values. Could he make the transition from a meaningless freedom in a meaningless world to a meaningful freedom in a meaningful world? Whether or not the inner recesses of his thought did move in that direction, the widely noted philosophy he has set in motion, with its focus on freedom and responsibility, should help free us from the bondage of any form of biological or naturalistic determinism. Despite his denial of God, we could all learn something from that."

Despite my long account of my discussion with Sartre, and although the hour was late, Albert seemed in no hurry to depart. Finally, after some moments of silence, he spoke: "Howard, you say that you have read my novels. Since you have spoken to Sartre, you have probably noticed his influence in my writings." Then he quoted from his novel *The Plague*, in which one of the leading characters, Dr. Rieux, says:

> "Since the order of the world is shaped by death, mightn't it be better for God if we refuse to believe in Him and struggle with all our might against death without raising our eyes toward the heaven where He sits in silence.
>
> Tarrou nodded.
>
> "Yes. But your victories will never be lasting; that's all."
>
> Rieux's face darkened.
>
> "Yes, I know that. But it's no reason for giving up the struggle."
>
> "No reason, I agree. Only now can I picture what this plague must mean for you."
>
> "Who taught you all this, doctor?"
>
> The reply came promptly: "Suffering."

Camus continued: "When I first met Jean-Paul Sartre, I agreed we should leave God out of the discussion, although I have always left open the possibility of something higher than man. To me, it was simply nothing we could ever know definitively, so at the very least we must live as if we are alone. There is no ultimate frame of reference, no absolute, eternal truths—only individual men and women doomed to pick their way through a meaningless existence, doing what they can to give it some essence or meaning. As Sartre himself put it: 'Subjectivity must be the starting point'—the point of departure for all authentic philosophizing by the existing individual that is cast into a world which is, on the face of it, meaningless and absurd.

"Sartre and I have always shared the same concerns in that we have shifted the focus of value from God to man himself." Camus also said he agreed with Heidegger's description of man's confrontation with existence and the discovery of oneself as an existing being, a state that he called "forlornness," or to use the title of one of Sartre's own novels, a feeling of "nausea."

"Contrary to popular belief," Camus said, "I have never called myself an existentialist, but I have always identified with this sense of isolation and powerlessness in the midst of an alien universe. And like Sartre, I have sought to find morality in the face of despair and the prospect of a Godless universe. As I once told a group of Dominican monks, 'I share with you the same revulsion from evil but I do not share with you your hope in God. And I continue to struggle against this universe in which children suffer and die.'"

Camus stopped to think as he swirled tea in his glass and peered over the rim. "I still owe much to him despite everything, but I now find his attempt to find meaning in life lacking. I am no longer satisfied with his answers."

I could see so many differences between these men, now, despite their often being compared to one another— often it seemed that one could not even be mentioned in a sentence without the other. Camus was a handsome man, quiet, almost shy, who seemed to treat each of our visits as a formal occasion. He was always polite and perhaps even stiff. Sartre, on the other hand, seemed far more abrasive, more confident. He lacked Camus' sense of modesty. But as I sat there replaying my visit with Sartre, an even larger gulf appeared between them: Sartre thought that he had found his answers; Camus had not, and perhaps he never would. For Camus, the mystery of life was a constant struggle, a continuous fight to find truth, forever elusive, yet always calling for him to try once more.

Finally we both stood, and after stretching a bit, Albert took a step toward me and said, "Please, tell me it is not true, that you are leaving soon."

I replied, "Yes, I am afraid that what you have heard is true. Next Sunday evening, I return to Ohio."

There was a moment of silence, then he said, "Howard, I am not a sentimental man, but I want you to know that your sermons and our all too few conversations have meant a great deal to me. In church last Sunday, several people told me that you might return next summer. Is it true?"

I replied simply, "Dr. Williams and the committee have invited me."

Chapter Seven

A few years later, I again served at the American Church for six or eight weeks. I renewed many acquaintances and friendships. Among them was Albert Camus. My first week back in Paris, I think we lunched together two times.

I will never forget the Bastille Day parade. I invited Albert to my guest apartment at the Church. The Church was on the parade route, so we would have a good view of the festivities. We watched the bands and the military marching on the street below, surrounded by hundreds of applauding Frenchmen. Camus explained to me the significance of Bastille Day. It is a commemoration of the day in 1789, when the people of Paris rose up against the reactionary government of Louis XVI and took the Bastille by storm. It was sort of a symbolic affair, because it was the people's first experience of freedom.

"Before the second World War, there were always parades and music and dancing in the streets. But during the German occupation the celebrations were no longer allowed. After the war, it took a few years before the parades resumed. Still, ever since, the celebrations have not been the same. They are more somber now. You can sense it."

As we sat back, Camus admitted that he had become keenly interested in the causes of human conflict. He acquired his interest during the war and reread Thucydides and Herodotus in search of an answer. They both wrote a good deal about the quarrels between the Athenians, and the Greek–Persian wars, and the treaties they had made and broken. The causes of human conflict troubled them even then, despite the fact that war was as normal as sleep in ancient Greece and was taken for granted as a part of everyday life.

Camus said that the search consumed him. He read voraciously, charting the progress of war through the centuries, moving on to Homer's *Iliad* and the long bitter way at Troy. Then he studied the events of the Peloponnesian wars and Hannibal's second Punic war and even the war of 1877 between the Russian and Ottoman empires. Lastly, he made a study of the first and second World Wars, concluding that when people organize in states, they are moved to fight wars. "The competition for power," he said, "is the most fundamental cause of war. In fact, war itself is nothing more than the armed competition for power."

"But," he continued, "I have concluded that power in itself is neutral, neither evil nor good. The purpose of power is to acquire the capacity to bring about goals or desired ends, and generally nations want power because they are afraid. They are afraid of someone else. They are afraid of another nation, fearful that their trade will be taken away. This built-in fear of every other nation causes them to build up arms and seek as much power as they can get—not only for what it can do but for power itself.

"The desire for power is unattractive, deplorable, and regrettable, but it is also inescapable. Nations want power because they want security, and that almost always leads to domination in some form."

The cheers outside became louder and interrupted his thoughts, when, following close behind a group of tanks, an open touring car drove by slowly with General De Gaulle propped up on the back seat, waving to the people. Suddenly, in the face of what Camus had just said, I recognized that I had become part of the celebration of freedom by cheering the weapons of war. If freedom is gained only by violent revolution and must be celebrated, I wondered if what Camus said was true. Are war and dominance inevitable, another cycle of life that cannot be avoided, only survived?

This was not idle speculation. It was yet another issue that eventually brought us back to the question of theodicy. For example, one Old Testament name for God is "Lord God of Hosts" which could, not inaccurately, be translated today to "General of the Armies" (which, incidentally, was the exact rank bestowed on George Washington and later on John J. Pershing.) Certainly, the Old Testament is filled with stories of horrific wars that were apparently sanctioned by God. Even Jesus himself said he came not to bring peace but a sword.

After several hours, the parade ended. Slowly the crowd dispersed. The streets emptied. We were deep in thought. After some silence, Albert asked the all-important question. He was serious and seemed to be deeply concerned.

He asked, "How do Christian philosophers and theologians deal with the problem of theodicy?"

I paused, considering how to best approach such a daunting topic. I replied, "I have asked myself that very question many times. Sooner or later, every one of us asks how or why God can be loving, exercise omnipotence, and, at the same time, permit evil and misfortune to thrive in the world as we know it."

Camus replied, "That is exactly the question that we ask today and that people across the centuries have asked."

I continued, "There was a time when I thought that I knew the complete answers but, the day that I stood in Auschwitz, the prognosis for better understanding seemed all the more elusive. The critique for each of the explanations demolished them. So, I, too, am a seeker of truth.

"Of course, theologians and philosophers have been trying to solve this problem for centuries. As you well know, there was a seventeenth-century philosopher by the name of Liebnitz, who believed that this is the best of all possible worlds because it was impossible for God to choose any other. According to him, it was impossible to have a world devoid of evil. God uses sin, evil, and suffering as a means of magnifying and enhancing his own grace and glory. The reasoning is that if God had not permitted sin, he would have been prevented from displaying his own benevolent mercy. This would have frustrated the manifestation of the divine glory as well as the good that comes to man through divine grace. Evil is necessary for the enrichment of life's complexity, just as painting requires contrasting hues and colors and musical compositions require some assonance. A full life requires a diversity of experience. Furthermore, men and women emotionally mature through suffering. The experience makes them stronger.

"Granted, such explanations appear forced and superficial. It is not much comfort to a man wracked with cancer that into each life a little rain must fall in order to find personal enrichment—that is, if he even survives."

Camus responded, "I am reminded of Voltaire's satiric novel, *Candide*, in which the hapless Candide falls from one outlandish and ridiculous evil to another, all the while maintaining that this is 'the best of all possible worlds.'"

I had to agree. Another idea we discussed was the aesthetic or totality theory of evil, the idea of the goodness of the whole. According to this theory, evil—both moral and natural—is something that appears to exist from our limited human point of view. If we could survey the entire history of the universe, from the standpoint of the whole, we would see that ultimately all things are interconnected or related so as to produce the greater harmony or good.

Here Camus stepped in to continue, "This understanding of good and evil was one of the basic teachings of the ancient Greek philosophy known as Stoicism. Central to this philosophy was its concept that a divine logos, or reason, directs the unfolding of the cosmos and history. A divine reason and purpose encompasses all that exists. Stoicism believes in the ultimate unity, harmony, and goodness of the universe. In the Stoic's view, everything is governed by divine reason and law. The judgment that there is evil in the world follows from our ignorance of the whole and of our insensitivity to the rationale and purpose of the whole of all things.

"From the standpoint of the all-embracing knowledge of God, all things are good and beautiful and reflect an ultimate order and purpose even when all that is available to our view is disgusting and pernicious. It behooves one, then, to attune his mind and soul to the divine logos and appreciate the ultimate harmony of things. In this way a person cultivates a divine perspective and is freed from anxiety and fear, for he has confidence in the rule of reason. In this sense, knowledge is a step toward salvation. Of course, there follows from all of this the well-known Stoic doctrine of resignation of things to their allotted roles. The idea received eloquent expression in Epictetus:

> "Remember that you are an actor in a play, and the playwright chooses the manner of it: if he wants it to be short, it is short; if long, it is long. If he wants you to act a poor man you must act the part with all your powers.... For your business is to act the character that is given you and act it well; the choice of the cast is Another's.

"Epictetus encourages us to always have at hand a piece like this one by Cleanthes, 'Conduct me, Zeus, and thou, O Destiny. Wherever you have fixed my lot, I follow cheerfully. Did I not, wicked and wretched must I follow still.' The Stoics represent a long tradition of reflective people constrained to opt for logos, God, and neutrality rather than face God's abandonment of the world and experience rational existence."

Another possible solution I put forth was the idea of free will. "Since God created men and women with free will, which includes the power to choose between good and evil, then suffering is not due to any inability or injustice on God's part. It is the fault of people who misuse their freedom and create their own hardships. Having given humanity freedom of choice, there is no reason to blame God for the results of that freedom."

To this, Camus responded, "Then I suppose the question becomes 'how can God have given people free will knowing, as he must, that we would misuse it so badly.' Would everyone be better off if we had less freedom? I tend to think that this is not so, but perhaps it is fair to ask why God made us as we are. If we had been made with a little more desire to do good, and a little less to do wrong, we might be better off."

I said, "The traditional answer to that argument is: 'God has allowed our moral freedom to provide some sort of test of our virtue.' If we were all naturally good, there would be little question of good versus evil. Then there is the familiar defense: 'Doesn't the world need some sort of evil so that we can recognize good?'"

"Perhaps," Camus said, "But I can't believe that we need the amount of evil and suffering in the world that we now have."

"No," I said. I had to agree with him. Even if we accepted God as omniscient and omnipotent and laid the blame for suffering on people's own choices, we still would not have solved the problem of evil. The free-will defense, at best, seemed to be only a partial solution.

"Again, the story of Job seems relevant here," Camus said. "Would this be tolerable on a human scale? For example, what would we say of a father who spanked his children to test their loyalty to him?"

"No, that certainly doesn't seem tolerable at all," I replied.

Then Camus asked, "Is this not a case where Christians are tempted to refer to 'God's mysterious ways?' We cannot begin to understand God's ultimate purpose, so we must simply accept what he does without question?"

I nodded in agreement. "This to me contradicts the Christian belief in a rational universe. In all the arguments that we have discussed, a belief in God's omnipotence and perfect justice has been a matter of rational belief. With reference to 'God's mysterious ways,' we breech the rational tradition. We admit that we cannot know about God—we cannot even understand or think rationally about these matters."

"Yes, you solve the problem of evil by discarding the discussion altogether," Camus laughed.

"Albert, people through the ages have asked whether our human tragedies and misfortunes are punishments from the hand of God. Sometimes, people have concluded that this is so, that even in this life, God directs good fortune toward the righteous and punishes the unrighteous with misfortune. This is the theory, as you remember, that was presented by Job's friends—either suffering is delivered directly on the sinner or on his descendants—this idea has never totally been discarded by the popular mind. But both forms of the theory were explicitly rejected by Christ."

Albert replied, "I certainly agree with you that all suffering is neither a direct result of sin nor a just recompense for it. In fact, in *The Plague* I had a Jesuit priest preach a violent sermon in the cathedral on the theme that the plague had been sent by God to punish the town of Oran for its wicked ways."

I remembered the story well. One day early in spring, a rat comes out into a city street and dies. In the following days, rats begin to litter the streets until the city sanitation employees are overworked with the disposal of dead creatures. Speculation about the phenomenon exists, but not even the doctors take it seriously. After all, this is the 1940s; society supposedly has great control over its environment. Citizens die at the rate of thirty per day for two straight days before the townspeople realize that they have a serious problem. When they realize that there is a plague, the priest gives a real fire and brimstone sermon:

> If today the plague is in your midst, that is because the hour has struck for taking thought. The just man need have no fear, but the evil doer has good cause to tremble. For the plague is the flail of God and the world His threshing-floor, and implacably He will thresh out His harvest until the wheat is separated from the chaff. There will be more chaff than wheat, few chosen of the many called.

"Following this sermon, a three-year-old boy comes down with the plague," Albert explained. "On the night of the child's death, Father Paneloux stands on one side of this child victim throughout the night. As the day breaks, the child seems to improve. This is a temporary remission, however. The disease returns with increasing intensity until indescribable agony extinguishes the spark of life. Thus, the plague claims its first innocent victim. Silence after the death rattle seems to come from deep within the cosmos. It is senseless by all standards."

"This certainly is a misconception of the cause of suffering and misfortune, and we must reject it out of hand," I said, and Camus nodded. "We may not fully understand God and the universe, but we can accept that God is not behind the scenes pulling the strings on every single event directly—rewarding the good and punishing the bad."

"I can certainly agree with that," Camus said.

I told Albert a story from the Enlightenment, in which the question of evil as punishment was presented with quite a problem. An earthquake struck on a Sunday morning, just as people were in church worshiping. The European community found itself in great confusion, considering the fact that the pious people were more likely to be killed then the atheists who had drunk themselves to sleep on the bench. "In this case, does it make any sense to say that God is punishing or testing their faith? What could justify a punishment that killed the innocent children and spared the guilty? What could justify a 'test' in which people are killed just to see if they are still faithful?"

Camus said, "Now, Howard, I am anxious to know your thinking on this problem."

I replied, "I think that nearly all of the difficulties which most of us feel in connection to this topic arise because of the fact that omnipotence is ascribed to God. I think it is important, therefore, to make sure that omnipotence is rightly understood." I talked about a book C. S. Lewis had written a few years earlier entitled *The Problem of Pain.* He said, "If God were good, He would wish to make His creatures perfectly happy, and if God were almighty, He would be able to do what He wished. . . ."

Continuing, I said: "I think we make a good beginning if we reject the notion that omnipotent means the ability to do anything. I know that the Bible scripture tells us, 'with God all things are possible,' but this statement assumes 'if they are not self-contradictory.' Some people may ask if God is able to make a rope with only one end, or a circle square, but these questions are meaningless. God's omnipotence means power to do all that is intrinsically possible. In other words, you may attribute miracles to God, but not nonsense.

"The fact that God cannot accomplish that which is self-contradictory does not in any way contradict the notion that he is also all powerful and able to accomplish his will. This is a significant insight. It represents the central tradition of Christian philosophy as stated by Thomas Aquinas: 'Nothing which implies contradiction falls under the omnipotence of God.'

"It has long been believed that God is limited by the laws of logic. If it is nonsense to make triangles in which the sum of their interior angles is greater than 180 degrees, it is equally nonsensical to expect God to create beings without the dangers inherent in their createdness. Even God cannot create an interdependent community of persons without also producing a situation in which evil spreads. In other words, God cannot create an independent thing and still have complete control over it or limit it. For example, we cannot have water that quenches our thirst but does not drown people. It is impossible to have fire that will warm our homes but not scorch our flesh. Nor is it possible for God to create minds that are free, yet not capable of evil. This is not to say that createdness necessitates evil, but what we affirm is the notion that it is absurd to expect even God to make creatures who lack the characteristics and the possibilities of both good and evil."

Albert nodded, "So far I am with you, keep going."

"Let me put it another way. What is affirmed is the notion that it is absurd to expect even God to produce creatures who lack the characteristics of created beings. Such created beings have the ability to perform that which is good and loving, but they are also capable of producing that which is evil.

"It is my contention that since we live in a world that is both good and evil, the world in which we live is not already made but is in the process of being made. Since this is a creation that is being made, we ought to expect what we find—namely incompletion and imperfection. We live in a universe that is not complete. Thus, while we dare not deny the reality of pain and suffering and anguish, we need not attribute them to the direct will and purpose of God. Unless of course we succumb to the fallacious idea that God is omnipotent in the crudest sense of the term."

Camus was excited, when he said, "This sounds very much like Sartre's philosophy in which man defines his own nature. What we decide we decide for all mankind. What we do, we do for mankind. We are all involved in mankind and each of us is responsible. Only in responsible commitment can authentic living be found and an essence of man evolve. We on the ethical plane are in a creative situation and the finished product, whatever that might be, will have to be judged in terms of the values evolved along the way."

I continued, "Not seeing ourselves as active participants in our world causes great difficulties for some people. For instance, when a mother loses a child to a painful disease and is permitted to think that God wished for the child to suffer. The only reason that we have any such idea is the mistaken notion that God is not only the chief creative principle in all things but also is the immediate, sole cause of what takes place in the world."

"May I suggest that there is a second question that we should ask," Camus said. "And that is, what are we going to do about the suffering? How are we going to respond? Suffering is a given. We cannot escape its existence. It is how we deal with the suffering that defines who we are. We are free. We choose to either succumb to our reality or rebel and strive for happiness."

I was pleased with what Camus had said. I just had to add my own thoughts. "Let tragedy and misfortune lead us to God in order to straighten our own lives, our thinking and living. In other words, let the fact that we live in an imperfect world lead us to repent.

"We can begin by changing ourselves, and in so doing we can hope to change the world. Repentance is an active response, a turning toward God, a change of heart and of ways. We need to turn from our petty, narrow, self-centered concerns and preoccupations and work to evoke God's kingdom. We must commit ourselves as free men and women to do what we perceive as God's will. God desires and needs the cooperative efforts of human beings if his will of perfect goodness is to be realized.

"I have always opposed the picture of God as human dictator or tyrant controlling everything without active sharing on the part of his children. On the contrary, we have every reason to believe that God depends on the cooperation of his creatures. His plan and his purpose are made real in and through human decisions and not by an arbitrary feat on his part."

Camus asked, "Then what is left of God's omnipotence? Are we arguing for a finite God?"

"Not at all. Omnipotence should and does mean that God has the power to accomplish his will not in spite of but through the decisions of his people. His transcendence lies in his capacity to work toward the accomplishment of his purpose with resources that are adequate in the long run to meet and overcome every obstacle to the end that he has in view. For us to truly live we must not withdraw from the struggle against all that is wrong in the world. We must rejoice in being co-creator with God in the advance toward his kingdom of love and peace on earth and good-will toward men.

"What God does in the world like this is enter into, identify himself with, and suffer in the situation as a whole. He invites us to join him in the struggle against wrong and social injustice. He is neither remote from the world nor untouched by our feelings of pain and suffering, the horror of our wrong doings, wrong thinkings, and wrong speakings. God is here in the midst of it all sharing his creatures' anguish, suffering with us the consequences of our sins, and urging us to positive action. The point is this: In the midst of our pain and suffering, God is with us. God is on our side. God's plan is to bring us out of all manner of darkness and to deliver all of mankind from everything that enslaves and defeats us."

Camus mused: "This, I take it, is the basic deliverance of sound Christian Faith as well as the main impetus of Biblical thought. To me, this is the best explanation for God's relationship with pain and suffering, especially the troubles of innocent people. I believe that this is the answer to the problem of theodicy. . . . Howard, have you read my essay 'The Myth of Sisyphus'?"

Like many people, I had. According to the Greek legend, Sisyphus was a king who offended Zeus. As punishment, he was forced to roll an enormous boulder to the top of a steep hill. Every time he reached the top, the rock would roll down again forcing Sisyphus to start over again and again, for the rest of eternity. "This story might be called the tragic impasse of the human condition. Man is free to choose, but he knows that he is always going to be subject to error. Man is thrown into a finite existence, bounded at each end by nothingness. An existence that is engulfed by short life, risk, absurdity, and the frailty of human reason."

Camus nodded, "I believe there are several ways in which man has tried to deal with his situation. First, he has used reason. He has tried to understand the world in which he lives, but the world has no ultimate meaning, so there is nothing to understand. Reason can do nothing to help man. It is pure wishful thinking. Man has made a second attempt to understand the meaning of life—he has used religion. I have always believed that religion is also incapable and that man is always alienated from himself and the world. We do not live forever. We must, therefore, simply try to live a good life despite the fact that life itself may be devoid of meaning."

To me, this was the startling truth underlying Camus' philosophy: Despite it all, Camus was an optimist about the condition of man. He believed that while life is absurd it is also precious.

Then Camus began relating the types of men that he believed could be used as models for living. They are men who accept life as absurd and yet love it to its fullest despite its limits. What made them great men was that they lived life passionately.

"The first of these models is Don Juan. He has an appetite for love and life. He lives his life to its fullest. The next I call the actor. The third is the conqueror. But the greatest of them all is Sisyphus. His hopeless and useless task was, in the opinion of the gods, the worst of any punishment that they could inflict on man. But why did they punish him? Sisyphus, having died, was permitted by the god of the underworld to return briefly to the world of the living. After which, he failed to honor his word and return to the land of the dead. Sisyphus is a great hero because of his disdain for the gods and his love of life.

"But," Camus continued, "his punishment although useless is not meaningless. The glory of man is expending all his substance and existence to achieve precisely nothing. Sisyphus, constantly struggling to the top of the mountain and yet knowing that he will never attain his goal, continues to try. This perseverance is his greatness. If man had no free will, Sisyphus' punishment would be meaningless. But while knowing that he cannot achieve his desired end, he continues to push the rock up the hill. When it falls, he simply turns back down the mountain to start anew."

As I listened, I could see the wisdom of what Camus said. It was this perseverance that I so admired in him. Despite all his experiences—his poverty, his illness, the horrors of the Nazis—he never seemed to give up. He was sad, to be sure, but beyond his writings and our discussions of the despair of man, there lay some hope, some optimism. There was a beauty that transcended all the misery. Man has only one reality, his life, and he must live his life while still accepting his limits.

While I disagreed with Camus' belief that life has no meaning beyond itself, I could not help admiring his belief that the fundamental reason we should live life fully is that man has a duty to be responsible. With all of our strength, we should work for the happiness of others. Camus believed that man is not a puppet, carried along by the inevitable process of living—he is free. He can choose to defy the absurd. He can combat social injustice wherever he finds it. There are heroes in life as well as anti-heroes, and these are in Camus' writings—the conqueror, the rebel, the good doctor combating the plague—these all hint at the heroic quality of man.

In effect, this is a Christian doctrine of the acceptance of the evils in the world and the Christian affirmation that one does not submit to injustice and suffering. To the contrary, Camus was calling for constant and active revolt against all kinds of injustice and suffering. True, he said that these heroes are absurd heroes. They know that they live in an absurd world. They know that they are problematic and will die. They know that the world is imperfect. They know that everything in the world has free will but with this freedom comes despair. But through it all, Camus said, "I am optimistic about man." He was pessimistic about human destiny but optimistic about man.

"We know evil exists. We have established that fact beyond all doubt. The important question is: 'Is there reason to hope?'" Then Camus quoted the words of Dr. Rieux in *The Plague*:

> Since the order of the world is shaped by death, mightn't it be better for God if we refuse to believe in Him and struggle with all our might against death without raising our eyes toward the heaven where He sits in silence.

"You know these lines of *The Plague*. . . . I have quoted them to you before, but do you know what I had in mind when I wrote them?"

"My impression was that you were concentrating on the suffering of the innocent. One would expect fear and terror in Oran in the face of the plague, but instead we find only longing for loved ones. As you said, 'Reunion is only the exception and happiness only an accident that has lasted.'"

Camus seemed amused by my interpretation. I wondered if I had perhaps given the wrong answer, so I asked, "How would you describe what you were trying to say?"

"I was trying to say that there are at least three responses humanity can make to the plagues of human experience. First, a man may commit philosophical or physical suicide. That is, a person may simply yield to the sheer impossibility of the situation. Second, he may develop a nihilistic posture, characterized by the asthmatic old Spaniard who spends his days transferring dried beans from one pot to the other. (That alternative doesn't make life any better or any worse.) Last, and possibly most important, I tried to present the alternative of revolt, represented by the sanitation squads who go out and bury the dead bodies. Even around the collective funeral pyres, man responds to the inner flame of comradeship in the service of human survival.

"To me this is all there is—simply going on living. The only hope that I can offer is simply to live. Repetition, grilling each day with the pure act of living. Starting over again until death, that is all there is. Yet, Howard, I sense deep within that something is missing. Is there more?"

"We have talked about the evil of men, the terrible things that we do to each other, but I truly believe that if anything is to be our undoing, it is pessimism. We have only two choices: despair, which leads to total destruction, or hope, which is the certainty of eternal salvation. In the final analysis, only a profound faith will give us that kind of hope. For only such a faith sees behind the passing scene to that which is permanent. He who has that kind of faith says with the psalmist: 'Why art thou cast down, O my soul, and why art thou disquieted within me? Hope thou in God.'

"If Jesus meant what he said when he taught us that the Kingdom of God is among us, then perhaps it is God's ultimate will that mankind build its faith to the point that it can change the world, no matter how many thousands of years it may take.

"Albert, always keep in mind that Christian belief is more than a set of tenets or beliefs to guide our conduct.

On the contrary, Christianity is the measure of our whole being, and, as such, it is a process that consumes a lifetime. In practical terms, this means that no matter how despairing, how ugly, how foreboding, how disparaging, how tragic, or how devastating the conduct of mankind proves to be, Christians never lose hope. This is because 'Christ died to make men holy, we must live to make men free.'

"There are two facts that Christian people look on which give them hope. First, they recall what the Risen Lord has done for their lives. If you could have asked the Apostle Paul why he was hopeful, he might have replied something like this: 'I remember the kind of man I was before Christ came into my life. I was a hard-boiled Pharisee, stiff-necked, censorious, sharp in my judgments. I hounded innocent people to their deaths. Then Christ came into my life and melted down my harshness. He surprised me. He made me into a new creature. Where I once hated, I now love. Where I once was impatient, I am now willing to suffer to be kind. Where I once was haughty, I now can humble myself. And what Christ did for me, he does for others. He changes Zacchaeus from a chiseler into a philanthropist. He transforms an adulteress into a person of purity.' Then, I believe, Paul would have added, 'I have hope, because what Christ did for Peter, for Zacchaeus, for an adulteress, and for me, he can do for anyone.'

"The second fact that gives Christians hope is the knowledge of God. The world is in the control of a being of infinite wisdom and power. He is not going to fail or be discouraged until he has brought about that 'better' which he has in store for us. Why believe this world of ours is under the control of a moral intelligence? Because it would have gone to smash long before now if it wasn't.

"The New Testament recognizes, time and time again, the power of evil in our world. But, we know that God is with us in the struggle against those evils, and that Christ Jesus has already overcome them. We can then, with hope, join the fight for peace, security, and justice in our world, for God fights with us. The final victory is not in our hands, but in God's, and he will prevail."

"It seems to me," Camus said when I had finished, "that you and I are not so very different."

"Why do you say that?"

"Because, in the face of despair, we have both found reason to hope. We both, above all, value life."

Chapter Eight

One day toward the end of my summer in Paris, the concierge's wife prepared us another supper. One of their daughters served it to us in my apartment. Camus and I were going to take a ride that afternoon but, after we finished our meal, we could not bring ourselves to leave. We chose instead to sit and enjoy the view of the river. We were both relaxed enjoying the weather and our full bellies, when Camus broke the silence: "Howard, do you perform baptisms?"

For a moment, I thought I was going to fall off my chair—the great Camus asking about baptisms. "Yes, Albert, I do," I answered with some tension and surprise.

"Why, what is the significance of this rite?"

I had become quite accustomed to his questions and by

now we had developed a kind of routine. Still, there was something different about this question. He seemed more than merely curious, rather contemplative, as if this question was more personal to him.

"Baptism is not necessarily a supernatural experience," I began. "The important thing is not the heavens opening up or the dove or the voice. Those are the externals, oriental imagery. Baptism is a symbolic commitment to God and there is a longstanding tradition and history involved."

"Yes, I remember some of it from my readings."

"First of all, let me say a word about why the average adult seeks baptism. I think, Albert, that you are a good example. You have said to me again and again that you are dissatisfied with the whole philosophy of existentialism and that you are privately seeking something that you do not have."

"Yes, you are exactly right, Howard. The reason I have been coming to church is because I am seeking. I'm almost on a pilgrimage—seeking something to fill the void that I am experiencing—and no one else knows. Certainly the public and the readers of my novels, while they see that void, are not finding the answers in what they are reading. But deep down, you are right—I am searching for something that the world is not giving me."

"Albert, I congratulate you for this. I think that I want to encourage you to keep searching for a meaning and something that will fill the void and transform your life. Then you will arrive in living waters where you will find meaning and purpose."

"Well, Howard, you have to agree that in a sense we are all products of a mundane world, a world without spirit.

The world in which we live and the lives which we live are decidedly empty."

"It does often seem that way," I conceded.

"Since I have been coming to church, I have been thinking a great deal about the idea of a transcendent, something that is other than this world. It is something that you do not hear much about today, but I am finding it. I am hearing about it here, in Paris, within the walls of the American Church.

"After all, one of the basic teachings that I learned from Sartre is that man is alone. We are solitary centers of the universe. Perhaps we ourselves are the only ones who have ever asked the great questions of life. Perhaps, since Nazism, we are also the ones who have loved and lost and who are, therefore, fearful of life. That is what led us to existentialism. And since I have been reading the Bible, I sense that there is something—I don't know if it is personal or if it is a great idea or powerful influence—but there is something that can bring meaning to my life. I certainly don't have it, but it is there. On Sunday mornings, I hear that the answer is God.

"You have made it very clear to me on Sunday mornings, Howard, that we are not the only ones in this world. There is something that is invisible. We may not hear the voice, but there is some way in which we can become aware that we are not the only ones in the world and that there is help for all of us."

Camus leaned forward until his elbows rested on his knees and said, "In the Bible, I have read about people who were not at all self-confident. Men who did not feel as if they had the world by its tail or that they had all the answers. Fact is, one of the things that I have noted in the Bible is that many of its chief characters were confused—just like the rest of us. We are on a pilgrimage. We are all seeking something, whether it is confidence or knowledge or something else entirely. I've read the Old Testament now at least three times and I have made many notes on it. In its pages I have found some people who were absolutely confused about life and what they should do and what God wanted them to do.

"There is Jonah, a guy who stood up and refused God. He didn't want to go to Nineveh! He didn't understand what it was all about. He felt that there was no chance for the Ninevites to be redeemed and that God was mistaken. Then there was Moses. God wanted him to go to Egypt to free his people, but Moses complained that he stuttered. He couldn't speak well and therefore no one would believe him. And then there was Isaiah. I have read Isaiah a number of times. When God wanted him—in the sixth chapter, I think—to go and work for him, Isaiah said, 'You have the wrong man! I am not worthy, I'm a man of unclean lips!' So even these great men were confused."

Then Camus said, "And I don't understand it to this day—this man Nicodemus!"

I was very pleased when he brought up Nicodemus. I got out the Bible and turned to the third chapter of the Gospel of John and we reread it. We discussed it. He said to me, "Now here is a wise man of Israel! He is seeking something that he does not have. I feel right at home with Nicodemus, because I too am uncertain about this whole matter of Christianity. I don't understand what Jesus said to Nicodemus, 'You must be born again.'"

I said, "Albert, let's think about this expression, to be born again, because we are moving back to the significance of baptism. What was Jesus' reply?"

Immediately Camus said, "Well you know what it was! He simply said that you must be born again! I know the exact words: 'Except a man be born of water and of the Spirit, he cannot enter the Kingdom of God,' whatever that is. And he said, 'That which is born of the flesh is flesh and that which is born of the Spirit is spirit.' And then Nicodemus said, 'I just simply marvel at it, that you must be born again.'"

"Well," I said, "let's think about this a little bit. Let me tell you what I feel down deep and see if I can make it clear. To me, to be born again is to enter anew or afresh into the process of spiritual growth. It is to wipe the slate clean, so to speak. It is to receive forgiveness. It is to receive forgiveness because you have asked God to forgive you of all past sins, so that the guilt, the concerns, the worries, and the mistakes that we have made in the past are forgiven and the slate is truly wiped clean.

"I don't know what the French term would be for a bond or an encumbrance, but the person who accepts forgiveness now believes that there is no mortgage, no encumbrance on you. The slate is clear, your conscience is clear. You are ready to move ahead and commit yourself to a new life, a new spiritual pilgrimage. You are seeking the presence of God himself." I was nervous and intense.

Albert looked me squarely in the eye and with tears in his eyes, said, "Howard, I am ready. I want this. This is what I want to commit my life to."

Of course, I rejoiced and thanked God privately that he

had come to this. I had a difficult time maintaining my composure. The man had been questioning me now for several years about Christianity and had attended services in the summer (possibly in the winter too, although he never indicated that he had.) He had heard my sermons on many occasions and I knew he had studied almost the whole Bible. Perhaps I should not have been shocked, but it did give me a sense of wonder and amazement that he would be considering taking this kind of step toward Christianity. Yet for some reason, I was unable to commit myself fully to the idea. "But Albert," I said, "haven't you already been baptized?"

"Yes," said Camus, "when I was a child . . . but it meant nothing to me. It was something done to me, no more meaningful than a handshake."

"Well, the baptism of a child is not performed because the child has faith in God or in Christ, which a baby clearly does not have. It is given because God loves the child and welcomes him into the family of God. The baptism begins a process in which you begin to grow, even as an infant, into a new life with which the gift has been given to you."

"But it seems right that I should be baptized now that I have spent these months reading and discussing the Bible with you. . . ."

I had to interrupt, though I could not express my full thoughts. Christian doctrine holds that one baptism suffices; there is no reason for re-baptism. Only if there is some doubt that a person has been given a valid baptism do we re-baptize, and we call it a 'conditional baptism.' So on one hand, I wanted to deny his request for baptism on the grounds that it wasn't necessary. On the other hand, I also sensed that Albert needed the experience. My compromise was to bring up the matter of joining a church and experiencing the rite of confirmation. That proved to be a mistake.

Right away, he jumped on me and said, "Howard, I am not ready to be a member of a church! I have difficulty in attending church! I have to fight people all the time after a service, even at your church. When I come to your church, when you are preaching, I leave before the service is over to get away from them all."

I understood that, but I had to stand my ground. "The time will come when you can get away from people who are seeking your autograph or wanting to hold conversations with you about your writings. Perhaps they will simply accept you into the community of men and women. This community will remind you constantly that you are not alone and that you are a member of a communion, a company of both the living and the dead, all of whom are in the presence of a living God. In any event, are you aware of everything that baptism entails?" I asked, trying to give a little.

Camus shrugged, "My experience is limited to my early church training and the little bit that you have told me," he said, recalling that baptism is a religious rite performed by a priest or minister on a baby. He puts water on the head of the child and blesses it. . . . It is a religious miracle of sorts, so that if the child should die, it would not go to hell. He said that beyond that, he knew very little.

"Yes," I said. The baptism is an outward and visible sign that an infant has been initiated into the fellowship of Christ's church. The child not only becomes a participant, but also becomes an heir to eternal life. That is to say, physical death will not end the gift which is given through baptism. "Jesus our Lord has, of course, given to the children a special place among the people of God. Jesus Christ said, 'Let the children come to me, do not hinder them, for to such belongs the Kingdom of God.'"

I went into more detail. I explained how the parents or sponsors bring a child to the baptismal font which in most churches is in the front of the church at the side of the railing or the altar. In the case of adults, they may approach alone. "The person then stands before the priest or minister as he addresses not only him but the entire congregation. . . ."

When I mentioned this, I noticed a frown appear on Camus' face, but I continued. "First the minister says, as he places his hand in the water and then places it on the forehead, that baptism is an outward and visible sign of a gift, the gift of the Spirit of God brought into the body and mind of the person being baptized."

I noticed Camus cringing again. He must have seen the questioning look on my face because he explained: "For me, baptism and confirmation would be a more personal thing, something between me and God."

"But baptism and confirmation are both a private and a public commitment to a life of Christ. They are a welcoming into the family of God, which is the church here on earth, both visible and invisible. At the end of the baptism, the minister confirms you as a full and responsible member not only of the family of God, which is personal, but also of the church, which is a community."

Camus shook his head, leaning back in his chair, obviously disappointed. "I cannot belong to any church," he said. " Is this not something that you could do? Something just between us...?"

I cannot say that I blamed him for his hesitation. Camus was one of the most famous Frenchmen alive. His popularity, based on his writings, touched the disaffection the people of France were feeling after the war and which reached all institutions, including religious ones. A public display of this sort would have all of France abuzz, and, no doubt, many of his fans would feel betrayed. But his trepidation was more than that—Camus, by his very nature, was a man who could never belong to an organized church. He was truly an independent thinker, and no matter how modified his feelings towards Christianity had become, he could never be an active member of any church.

"Perhaps, you are not quite ready," I said. As pleased as I was, I could not fully commit myself to the idea. I would be leaving in a few more days and he would have plenty of time to think and read to contemplate what he really wanted. He had learned much about the Christian faith—and I had learned much from him—but we still had so much more that we could gain from each other. This was a major decision for both of us, and I wanted to be sure that there were no doubts about his next step. With a few more months to stand back and analyze, we could both be certain that this was the right decision. I laid my hand on his and said, "Let's wait while you continue your studies."

Chapter Nine

Albert had asked if he could drive me to the airport, but some of the officials of the American Church had planned a luncheon for me on the day I was to leave. I asked Albert if he could meet me at the airport instead. I wanted to see him one last time before I left. I had a fine lunch, and I was grateful for all the effort put forth on my behalf. I made sure to thank everyone involved several times. As we drove to the airport, I thought of the conversation Albert and I had just a few days earlier. I wondered again if he was truly moving toward Christianity; I have always believed that no one is beyond the reach of God. His heart is open to anyone who looks for it, but still all this seemed too incredible to accept. Yet, the Albert Camus I had come to know, who had read the Bible over several times and with whom I had talked on so many occasions, overruled my doubts and surprise. Albert was far from a confirmed church member—I could never imagine him as an active member of any church—but given enough time, enough study, perhaps. . . .

We pulled into the airport parking lot and I was pleased to see that Albert had brought Jacques, Suzanne, and Nicolette in his car, joining the two carloads of other friends and staff come to see me off. I took turns shaking everyone's hands and saying goodbye with hugs all around for my few remaining minutes. Last in line was Albert. He hugged me and gave me a long look as if memorizing my face. Then he said, as if he knew what I was thinking about, "My friend, mon chéri, thank you. . . . I am going to keep striving for the Faith!"

As he said this, I wondered if I should have done as he asked, baptized and confirmed him. He was very close; I was becoming certain. Given a little more study, he would be ready, possibly even by next summer. I could baptize and confirm him if and when I returned. With another year of study and discussion, we could both be sure this was what he truly wanted. We could both know that it was the right thing for him. "Albert, I'm glad," I said, shaking his hand again and smiling. "And I am sure that you will find it." With that, I turned to board my plane and return to my family.

I remember the evening when the news brought word of his death. I was shocked, unable to move as they showed photos and summarized Camus' career, seeing this man I had come to know so well shown on the TV screen like so many other celebrities. This was a man I knew well, and it was hard to believe this actually had happened. I felt as if all the organs in my chest had collapsed. When I thought again of Albert Camus' last request of me, I sank a little lower.

I wondered again if I had made a mistake in not honoring his request. It seemed the right decision at the time, but had I realized that it would be my last chance to re-baptize him as he wanted, I might have decided differently. I was not sure what bothered me. I had implied that baptism was an event that usually only happens once, and I certainly wasn't worried for his soul. God had set aside a special place for him, I was sure. Camus was truly a decent, caring man and through all his writings and struggles with faith and philosophy, at his core was a genuine caring for the station of his fellow man.

Epilogue

Some years later, when I was again in Paris, I was being driven on a curving road in the French countryside. I was reading some notes as we drove, only occasionally looking through the window. I noticed the driver glance over his shoulder a few times nervously, as if he wanted to say something. "Do you know Albert Camus?" he asked when I made eye contact with him in the rearview mirror. I must have looked confused, so he added, "The writer?"

"Yes, of course," I answered after a moment, starting to realize that he did not assume that I knew him personally.

"Well, he was killed right over there," the driver said, pointing through the window to a tree some yards out from where the road curved.

"That's where the accident happened?"

"Yes sir," he said, slowing the car. "You want to see it?"

I nodded, and he stopped just off the road as I rolled down the window to look. I could see no visible damage to the tree, no missing bark or scars, at least from my vantage point. There was nothing spectacular about it at all, just an ordinary tree, but I couldn't remove my eyes from it. I don't know what I expected to see: some pieces of the car, bare ground, some evidence that this was truly the spot. It seemed the only tree around, so strange that his car would have hit it, a terrible coincidence.

"Would you like to get out and get a closer look?" the driver asked, and I shook my head slowly. "Are you certain?" he said, looking over his shoulder, "Many people stop here to look. . . ."

"No," I said. "I've seen all I need to." The driver pulled back onto the road and drove on with a shrug. I am sure he regarded my seeming indifference as disrespect, but it wasn't. I was lamenting my failure to restore faith in my friend, Albert, at least enough faith to stave off what to me was obviously suicide. Perhaps the depth of his despair was beyond anyone's ken, perhaps not.

Yet from death we can sometimes learn as much about ourselves as from the experience of life. For death can dramatize holiness more than words. So if I failed to restore faith in my friend, perhaps the memory and retelling of our conversations can help another overcome the understandable despair spawned by a world that often seems to alternate between evil and meaninglessness. God gave us dominance over the world as we know it. What have we done with that power?

THE MINISTER—
HEROES
AND FRIENDS

Author's Note

Memory is a mystery. Why do some people, some incidents, keep coming back to mind? Why do some people and incidents completely vanish from that same mind? Perhaps some moments are magic.

Magic moments follow no pattern, reason, or logic that can explain why they warm the heart or lift the spirit. The poet William Wordsworth called such moments "spots of time" in his chronicle of the growth of a poet's mind, "The Prelude." Such spots of time—memories—are common to us all. In the world of nature, Wordsworth found his spots of time. His magic moments were in waterfalls and moonlit mists. My spots of time, my particular magic moments, have come from people. Through their acts of kindness, people have helped me to see myself in new and often provocative ways. People I have met in my life's journey I now recall in these biographical essays.

My Mother

One morning when I was about nine or ten, I awoke with a toothache. When I told my mother about it, she asked if I wanted to stay home from school. I loved school and we were doing some interesting things, so I said no. After breakfast, I went off to school as I had on so many other days, but the tooth continued to throb. When I told my teacher, she said, "If it is still aching at recess time, you may go home."

When time for recess came, the tooth was still aching, so I was excused and went home. I rushed through the back door and into the kitchen, calling for Mother. She did not answer and was nowhere to be seen. She was not in the living room. I called down to the cellar, but she was not there either. Finally, I walked up the stairs to the second floor. I could hear her speaking softly. I bolted up the stairs and opened the door to her room ready to tell her of my aching tooth. As I started into the room, I saw that my mother was kneeling beside her sewing machine. Her eyes were closed, her hands folded. She was talking out loud to God.

Something told me not to disturb her, so I walked over to her bed and knelt down quietly to listen. I had heard people pray many times— my mother, my father, the minister—but this quiet prayer in my mother's bedroom was something different from everything else I had ever experienced. I stayed there, quietly listening to her.

When I arrived, she was praying for world peace. She prayed for the people of China. She prayed for the Japanese. She prayed for the missionaries. She prayed for President Roosevelt and the members of the Cabinet. Then she prayed for the members of Congress. She prayed for the church and the minister that he would be strong and do the will of God. I was deeply impressed.

After some hesitation, she prayed for my father. She prayed that he would be strengthened to continue to be a good leader in his corporation. Then she prayed for my oldest brother. When she began praying for my second brother, I realized that I would be next. Sure enough, she began praying for me. She prayed that I would be strong, physically and morally, and a good student. She prayed that I would learn to do the will of the Father. After she prayed for many others, including our maid, Mary, and her family. She prayed for herself. Finally, she said, "Amen" and stood up.

I was still kneeling when she saw me. She came over to me, put her arms around me and kissed me. I hugged and kissed her, and we walked downstairs together.

My toothache had vanished! I'll never know if it was a so-called sinus toothache that comes and goes, or a real toothache overcome by her prayers. What I do know is that the kindness my mother bestowed on every person in her prayers set the tone for the rest of my life. I experienced a presence that seemed to grasp my inner life and that remains with me today. I believe that this experience, this one moment, was the basis for an entire life filled with grace and faith.

The Berlitz Family

I wish I could say that I grew up without ever being conscious of prejudice, in myself or others, but virtually all of us are exposed to some prejudicial attitudes in our childhood. The issue is how we cope with this indoctrination of hate. I could easily have succumbed to these attitudes if not for the special sacrifice of a family who knew prejudice first hand.

Like most of my generation, I was taught very early that people were born different. When I was about three, I asked my mother why Mr. and Mrs. Armstrong, who lived across the street, didn't look like me. Mother answered, "When they were born, they did not get to the water trough in time to wash their faces and hands. You need to wash your face and hands very thoroughly." At the time, I accepted her explanation.

Many of the pupils in my class were what most people called "colored." I overheard a conversation between my mother and father about them once. Father said, "The company president called me into his office today. He asked me why we are not sending our three sons to a private preparatory school, where they wouldn't have to associate with colored children."

Mother said, "Well, what do you think about that?" They talked about it a while and came to a decision. Father said, "Our life includes relationships with all sorts of people, and our boys need to have that experience also. They will always be living, working, and associating with people of all different races and religions."

A music teacher at my school introduced me to another form of bias. Every Friday Mr. Jergens came to teach us to sing, right in our regular classroom. He was the only male teacher we knew, and when he came we were all glad, because we all loved to sing. All thirty of us were ready and waiting for our singing lesson, even Danny Rich. Danny couldn't carry a tune in a bucket, but he was always smiling, quick to laugh, and fun to be with. One day, Mr. Jergens asked Danny to stand on a chair seat and face the class. He teased Danny to make him try to sing, trying to get the melody right. The class laughed at Danny making funny faces while he tried.

Then, Mr. Jergens told Danny, "You can't sing because you are a Jew!" That bothered me, I didn't really know what he meant, but I thought maybe Danny did. So, to make him feel better, I asked him to come home with me after school. Mother had made cookies that day, so we ate cookies and played in the backyard. Two days later, he asked me to go home with him after school. Danny lived in a different section of town. The streets were full of shops, not houses and trees like ours. We passed many shops and stores before Danny turned to one and said, "I live here."

He was standing in front of a shop with big windows full of a variety of things. I saw a bicycle, an accordion, and a shelf full of watches. We walked into the store and Danny introduced me to his father. Then, we went straight through the shop and there, in the back, were the rooms where Danny lived. We had to play indoors because there was no backyard. That really made an impression on me—no backyard?

I'm sure there were many other instances that I can't recollect, but the first time it really affected me, I was in high school. At that time, we often went to dances at the country club. All of us would dance with as many partners as possible for as long as possible. To dance with more of the girls, we would cut in halfway through a dance—just tap on a dancer's shoulder and he would have to relinquish his partner to you. At one dance, I cut in on a particularly attractive girl and danced with her several times over the course of the evening. Finally, I asked if I could call her, to make a date. She said I could.

A week later I called her for a date. She set the time and I was at her house at 7:30 that evening. Her father met me at the door. "Come in, Howard." He said, "What courses are you taking at St. Raphael's?"

"Well, sir," I replied, "I don't go to St. Raphael's. I'm Methodist and go to Springfield High."

"Oh," was all he said.

I sat in the living room alone for several minutes trying to figure out what was going on. Finally Marie came in. I didn't have any sisters, but it looked to me like she had been crying. When we were in the car, I asked her if she would like to see a movie. She said, "I have to be home at 9:30—there's not time to see a movie. I have to be honest with you, my Father doesn't want me to ever date a Protestant boy."

"But how do you feel about it?" I sputtered.

"I like you. You're a good dancer. I would really like to be friends, but I guess it's impossible."

We took a short ride while she tried to explain and I tried to understand. Neither of us succeeded and so I took her home. The next day I asked my father about it. He said, "Mr. McNally was right. No Protestant boy or girl should ever date a Catholic girl or boy." That left me speechless—for the first time ever I questioned my father's judgment, but I got no further explanation.

Only a few months later, another issue came up about dating. Our local paper featured a new family in town, the Jaffas. Mr. Jaffa had purchased a small department store in our area and the article seemed very positive. Irene Jaffa, a beautiful girl just my age, started attending my school, and I lost no time making her acquaintance. Before long, I asked her for a date, and she accepted. At dinner that evening I told my parents I had a date at 7:00.

"Fine," my father said, "who's the lucky girl tonight?"

"I'm going out with a girl who transferred into our school a few months ago. Her name is Irene Jaffa."

My father gave me a stern look, "Do you know who her father and mother are?"

"No, but I saw a picture of their new store in the paper." I was puzzled by his question and more puzzled by his reaction. Both my father and mother demanded that I immediately go to the phone and cancel my date. They never did tell me why and it was years before I realized the extent of their bias.

All of these incidents were faithfully recorded in my mind, and fortunately, when I got to college, one particular experience erased most of the bias I had absorbed. It all began in the freshman dormitory. I was anxious to meet everyone, my neighbors especially, so a knock on my door brought me swiftly to my feet. It was the man from across the hall. He came in and introduced himself as Joseph Berlitz. He said, "We're playing bridge this afternoon at two o'clock, would you like to join us?"

I accepted eagerly; I liked bridge and thought I could keep up. Joseph, his brother Benjamin (they looked like twins), another student, and I made a foursome. We were evenly matched and had quite a good time. The brothers served Coke and pretzels, and the afternoon passed quickly. The next morning, when we all went off to our first classes, Joe stopped to invite me to play again at 2:00. I told him I had to study, but I accepted his offer to play the next day. As that afternoon drew to a close, Ben said, "Let's set it up to play every afternoon, from two till four or five!"

"Hey look, you two, I can't do that. I have to study, and when I'm not studying, I work out in the gym." They thought that was very funny. I was happy to amuse them, but I was starting to feel uncomfortable. The Berlitz brothers kept asking me and others to play bridge. They wanted to play six afternoons a week. How could they do that and get their work done? It wasn't fair! They had spent about ten years in private preparatory schools. They knew how to study, to organize—besides, they were just smart. I began to resent them and their brains. I had to study all the time if I expected to graduate, and I began to feel prejudiced against them and their money.

I tried to avoid the Berlitz brothers, until Joe came to me in early December with a different line. "When are you heading home for Christmas?"

I told him, "I'm not going home for Christmas."

He seemed surprised and asked, "Why not?"

I snapped at him a bit, saying, "Well, if you have to be so damn nosy, I can't afford it."

I put the conversation out of my mind, until about a week later when I received a letter with a Long Island postmark. Who do I know from Long Island?—Oh yes, those pesky Berlitz brothers came from Long Island. The letter, as it turned out, was from their mother. Mrs. Berlitz invited me to come to their house with Joe and Ben for Christmas and the long weekend! Wouldn't it be wonderful—I wouldn't have to stay in the lonesome dormitory and miss Christmas! What a nice lady!

I wrote the best letter I had ever written thanking her and accepting her invitation. The next time I walked to class with my neighbors, Joe asked, "Are you coming to our house?"

"Yes, I am. I wrote your mother right away."

"Fine! The car will pick us up tomorrow at four o'clock."

The next afternoon, a chauffeur driving the longest, biggest, Packard sedan I had ever seen stopped in front of our dormitory. He helped us with our suitcases and drove us to Bridgeport, Connecticut. From there we took the ferry across to Long Island. Then we drove about twenty miles to a large estate with fancy iron gates and the most beautiful house I had ever seen. As soon as we arrived, Ben and Joe removed the bags from the car, and Mr. and Mrs. Berlitz came out and hugged each of their sons and greeted me warmly, making me feel welcome.

We walked into that lovely home with its upstairs maids and its downstairs maids, its butlers and cooks, and at least twenty-five rooms. They showed me to my room with its own private bath. They did everything to make me feel at home, and I tried to act natural. After settling in and washing my face and hands, I went downstairs to the dining room where a butler seated me at the table. Before we started eating, the three Berlitz men put on little skullcaps, and the father opened the Torah and read from Deuteronomy and then they prayed together. It was a solemn experience for me. My own family had always said Grace before meals, but this was somehow different. After dinner we saw a home movie, Mrs. Berlitz played the piano, and we went to bed around ten o'clock.

The next morning, Saturday, as I walked downstairs, I could hear a big argument going on in the breakfast room. All the voices were polite but serious. I turned around and went back to my room and closed my door. About fifteen minutes later, I tried the breakfast room again, just in time to hear Mr. Berlitz say, "This is where we are going tomorrow morning."

Saturday was pretty exciting. The chauffeur drove us into Manhattan where we went to the theater for a matinee performance, next a light supper, and finally back to the house for a big party. Early Sunday morning, Mr. Berlitz knocked on my door and said, "Howard, we are having breakfast now. We will be leaving for church within the hour." I was glad I was already awake and dressed.

After breakfast, James, the chauffeur, and his wife, Mary, the Berlitzes, and I went all the way into Manhattan again, to Christ United Methodist Church on Park Avenue. The big Packard slid into a space by the door and all of us walked into the church together and sat in one pew, despite the fact that it was an era of prejudice and segregation that worked to keep us apart. So, there we were, together in God's house, worshipping in peace.

That Christmas weekend, the Berlitz family taught me a valuable lesson with their kindness. That family has been with me ever since, in my mind, protecting me from the prejudice that surrounds us all. I am grateful for their example. Years later, I told the story of that service to the pastor of a church on Park Avenue, the Reverend Ralph W. Sockman. He smiled and said, "I am not at all surprised." In time I came to realize what Christ meant when he said that he came not to abolish the law but to fulfill it.

Jack Caldwell

Early on the morning of September 12, 1933, I walked through the Phelps Gate and entered Yale University. I had eagerly anticipated this day for three years. The tuition had already been paid, but I would soon accumulate a debt of the sort that can never be repaid.

Several years earlier, I had been in college nearing the end of my freshman year. Late one night, I received a call from my father. "Son," he said, "I have some bad news to tell you. The stock market has taken all my capital—everything I had saved is gone. Some weeks ago I was dismissed, fired from the job I had held all my adult life. I thought then that we could get by on the stocks, but now they are gone too. We cannot afford to put you through college as we did for your brothers. I'm sorry."

I told him, "It's almost the end of school. I'm ready to come home. I will get a job and see if I can help us all."

"That is a wonderful plan, son," he told me ever so gently, "but there are thousands of people out of work right now. Just come home and we'll talk it over."

My father was a proud man, and I knew that it hurt him to tell me all this, but I was gratefully reminded in weeks to come that he was also a strong man. Over the following weeks, I heard stories of weaker men in similar situations who killed themselves rather than face a bleak future. I went home and got a job. It didn't pay very much, but in three years I saved enough to return to college. Over those three years, I worked so hard and for such long hours that I had no time to study. I realized that it would be very difficult to return as a sophomore.

I decided to start over at a new university. I applied to many colleges and wrote seeking scholarship help. Duke University offered me a small scholarship; Ohio Wesleyan offered me a bit more. Yale wrote to say that they would accept me as a transfer student, but it was their policy not to offer money to transfers. Yale did offer to give me financial aid for my second semester, if I did well in my first. I was glad to accept their conditional offer and was enrolled at Yale.

The next problem was finding a ride from Springfield, Ohio, to New Haven, Connecticut. My brother had a friend who was in charge of delivering new trucks from the factory in Springfield to their final destinations. He was kind enough to arrange a ride for me from the International Truck Company to Hartford, Connecticut; from there it would be easy for me to get a ride to New Haven.

I arrived a few days before classes to become accustomed to the area and to look for work, so it was early on the 12th of September that I entered through the Phelps Gate. As I walked around the campus, the Gothic architecture and the beautiful, new library impressed me. I wondered where I would be living and where I would go to classes. I saw the statue of Nathan Hale and read his life story. I considered all the famous people who had attended Yale and felt honored to be there. As I continued exploring the campus, a young man stopped me and said, "Good morning. Certainly you're not a new student here."

"Actually, I am new to Yale, a sophomore, looking forward to registration this week. I came a few days early to look for work and get acquainted with the campus. I am fascinated by all these grand buildings."

He began to tell me about the history of Yale and some facts about the buildings. He was most pleasant and accompanied me for a good while. Before he left me, he said, "Now, after you've registered, if you have any problems just come and see me. My name is Caldwell; I'm a senior here, graduating next June. If I can help you in any way, don't hesitate to ask."

I came to find out that he was a leading student at Yale; everybody knew him. He was a star halfback on the football team and editor of the *Yale Daily* news. Also, he was social secretary to the Provost, Vice-President of the University. Jack Caldwell was wealthy, but he was not resented. He was the most popular man on campus. He lived with two other students in one of the finest apartments at Yale. He seemed far above me, yet whenever I passed him, he always stopped, called me by name, and asked, "How are things going?"

I always answered, "Just fine, thanks. I am happy to be here and so glad to know you."

He repeatedly told me, "Don't forget, if I can help you in any way do not hesitate to call on me."

That first week, I found a job as a window dresser at Kresge's five and dime downtown. I could work as many hours as I wanted at forty cents an hour. When I registered, I spent my three-year savings: tuition, $400; meals, $375; my room, $125. I was left with no money for books and all the incidentals, so I desperately needed the job at Kresge's and as many hours as I could put in. And, whenever I was not working, I studied.

I liked my lectures on English literature, American history, and chemistry the best. I found all of them interesting, but after the lectures were the tests over what we had heard. Some of these tests came back to me with less than good grades. About the first of December, I had a letter from the Dean, asking me to come to his office at my convenience. I had no idea why he wanted to see me, but I called and set up an appointment. When the time came, I walked into his office, admiring the rich mahogany walls. There was a cheerful fire in the fireplace and Dean Warren was in a leather chair behind his desk. He got up immediately and came to me to shake my hand. He was wearing a tweed jacket and had his white hair parted in the middle—he seemed to personify academia. He was gracious and friendly, inviting me to sit in one of the beautiful leather chairs.

He said, "Mr. Mumma, your records have been sent to me, and I have been examining them. I am sorry to tell you that your grades are not measuring up to Yale standards. I wonder if you can explain your low marks? You are not doing as well as you did in your freshman year. You had excellent grades at your other university. I simply can't understand why you are not living up to the promise you showed there."

I told him that I was aware that I was not doing well and explained my changed circumstances, telling him of the hours I was having to work to stay at Yale.

He thought for a moment and said, "My friend, I understand what you are going through and that you have an explanation for your poor grades, but I am going to make a recommendation to you and hope you will take it in the spirit in which it is given. I recommend that you drop out of school and when you have sufficient funds to return, you enter one of the schools nearer to your home. It will not be as expensive and perhaps you will get along better. You must realize that you are competing with some excellent students here at Yale, and you are simply not doing as well as you must in order to stay in school here."

I thanked him for his concern and left. As I crossed the campus, I realized that the dean was probably right. Having been out of school for three years with no time to study would in itself have made returning difficult—add to that the number of hours I worked each week, and I simply could not do as well as I needed to. I felt depressed as I decided to pack my trunk. I called my father that night and told him what had happened. He said, "Well, it is understandable. You have had a hard experience. Why not come home for a while. We can talk about what to do next."

"Dad," I replied, "I'll call you in a few days and then take the milk train." The milk train ran from New Haven to New York City, leaving at midnight and stopping every five miles to pick up milk cans. Passengers paid $1.25 to arrive in New York at 5am.

On the night of December 7, my trunk and cases were ready to be taken to the station. I had eaten supper and prepared to leave New Haven at 11:00 to catch the milk train. As I sat in my room thinking about leaving Yale forever, I remembered that one friend would wonder what had happened to me. I decided I had to say goodbye and thank Jack Caldwell.

At about 8:00 I walked over to Berkeley College, climbed to the second floor, and knocked on Jack's door. A student who I didn't know answered the door. I asked him if I could see Jack for a few moments, but the student replied, "As you must know, Jack is a very busy man. I will be happy to give him a message, but I cannot disturb him. He is on a very tight schedule."

I could understand that and simply said, "That's all right." I turned and started down the stairs. All of the sudden, I heard Jack call out, "Hey, come back here. Come on in!"

The other student had disappeared, and I sat down with Caldwell to tell him the whole story—the grades, the dean, and leaving Yale. He thought about what I said for a few moments and then asked me some questions about what I wanted to do with my life and about my background and my thoughts. He was very deliberate. Twice I got up to leave, but each time he said, "Sit." and I did.

Finally he said, "Mumma, I want you to have lunch with me tomorrow."

"Mr. Caldwell, my trunk is all packed. I am taking the midnight train to New York and then going on home to Ohio. But, since you have been so nice to me and were so nice to me on my first day here, I couldn't leave without saying goodbye and thanking you."

He said, "Well, it won't hurt to stay one more day. It might even do some good. I want you to come and have lunch with me at Berkeley College tomorrow, at noon."

Finally I said, "All right," and I left. At the time I had no intention of going to lunch with Jack Caldwell; I just wanted to go home. Yet, as I walked back across the campus, I decided that he was right—one more day wouldn't hurt me. I decided I would stay for lunch, and that decision greatly affected the rest of my life.

Promptly at 12, I entered the leading college of Yale University. It was home to two hundred students and a number of professors. The dining room was modeled after those at Oxford with long oak tables and tall leather chairs. The walls were solid walnut and displayed paintings of famous British and American bishops, philosophers, and well known professors. Jack saw me as I entered the famous dining room and raised his hand signaling that I was to join him at a table with Dean Warren.

Jack stood as I approached the table, saying, "Dean Warren, you know Mumma, do you not?"

"Yes, I know Mumma," he said and then, to me, "please sit down." They started talking again and completely ignored me. I ate my lunch and said nothing, wondering why I had stayed. At last, during dessert, the dean turned to me. "Mumma, I have been thinking about you and your situation. I have decided that if you would like to stay here at Yale until Easter, I would be willing to review your progress at that time." A hint of compassion glinted in his cold, blue eyes.

I said, "Do you mean I could remain a member of the college?"

"Yes, and in good standing, but you are still on trial."

At that a strange feeling came over me, and something welled up in my throat. I asked to be excused and quickly walked out of the room and the College. Then I think I ran about ten miles, tears flowing and my heart filled with gratitude. Finally, late in the afternoon, I got back to my room and fell on my bed—sound asleep. It was much later when a knock on my door aroused me. I did not want anyone to see me and almost told the caller to leave, but something made me put on the light and open the door. Jack Caldwell was standing in the hall, smiling. I was a mess from crying and running, but Jack just kept smiling. He asked me, "Are you going to invite me in?" Once he was in and seated he asked another question, "Mumma, what are your plans for this Christmas vacation?"

I replied, "Mr. Caldwell, please accept my thanks. This has been one of the best days of my life. I don't know what all you did for me or how you got Dean Warren to change his mind, but I assure you I intend to stay here and study all through the Christmas holidays."

With that, he stood up and said, "That is the answer I wanted to hear. I want you to be at the tutoring school tomorrow at eight A.M." Then he walked out and closed the door.

Run by two brothers, the tutoring school helped wealthy students learn how to study and take examinations. The school saw these students through their years at Yale. It was a very expensive, private institution, not connected to the university. They claimed to have on file every test and final exam given over the previous twenty years. I was there the next morning, but had no expectations of joining. I knew I could never afford it.

I gave my name to the admitting office and the attendant said, "Please take a seat in that room with the others. We begin in fifteen minutes." I was surprised and said, "I would like to, but I cannot afford it."

He replied, "Young man, I will not mention money to you, and I would appreciate it if you do not mention money to me." I did not understand until several months later that Jack Caldwell had paid my tuition for six weeks at the school.

The instructors taught me how to study for chemistry, literature, and history, as well as many other things. I attended classes at the school for three hours every morning, seven days a week—including December 25, 1933 and January 1, 1934. After six weeks, I felt confident about studying on my own. I knew how to study, how to outline a lecture, and how to take examinations and pass them. I became like a new man and a new student. Three years later, I would graduate from Yale, with honors.

One day, after my Easter trial date, I received a letter from Dr. Seymour inviting me to tea. As we were drinking our tea, he said, "Jack Caldwell and I have been thinking about appointing his successor as my social secretary, since his graduation is approaching. You have been recommended for the position, and I am now offering it to you."

For the next two years, all of my expenses for tuition,

room, and board were paid by the university. In addition, I received a moderate salary. I don't know if I should call this a miracle, but it was to me. Jack Caldwell saved me in many ways. He was a good friend, and I loved him for all he had done. After graduation, he moved to an apartment in New York, but I visited him regularly. We remained good friends until his death.

Charles Sterling*

One warm October evening, I was sitting in my room in Connecticut Hall studying for a test. I smelled smoke and heard sirens. All of us, eager for some excitement, streamed out of the dorm and towards the smoke. "The theater is on fire!" someone yelled. I went back into the dorm to tell my friend, Charles Sterling.

"Charles! The theater's on fire, let's go see!" Nobody responded, so I set off without him. With a crowd of other students, I ran past the statue of Nathan Hale, across the Green, through the Phelps Gate, and on to the theater. There was already a throng of onlookers and firemen with their equipment gathered around the building. Patrons were running out of the first floor exits with smoke bil-

---

*   Charles Sterling is a pseudonym. His family requested that his proper name not be used.

lowing around them and pouring out of the windows above them. At these windows were some people who were apparently trapped on the upper floors.

While we were looking up at these poor, trapped people, we saw a painter's ladder being pushed through a theater window and balanced on the fifth floor window ledge of the Taft Hotel next door. A man climbed out onto that ladder and walked across to the hotel. He kicked in the window, and everyone on the ground cheered when we recognized that this man was Charles. We were all glad to see that he was safe.

At 6'2" and 200 pounds, he was one of the biggest men on the football team. He had a large, open face and massive hands. Despite his size, he was personable and friendly —well liked and admired. When I saw his massive form cross to the hotel window, I suppose I thought he would come down and join us on the street, but not Charles. Instead, he surprised us all by crossing back to the burning theater. A few minutes later, he reappeared carrying an old woman in his arms. He carried her across to the safety of the hotel. Then he returned and took a young girl to safety. On his fourth trip across the ladder, we all began to shout at him—"Charles, Charles, save yourself!"

The flames were steadily growing higher. The heat was intense. Nobody thought that the fire department would be able to save any part of the building or the people inside. The cries of the trapped, burning people were hideous and hard to bear. As the flames grew and the cries heightened, others, including some firemen, encouraged Charles to stop his dangerous journeys; he had done enough. Charles heeded no one. He continued moving back and forth carrying a person with him on each trip to the hotel. On his seventeenth trip, heading back toward the theater, the ladder gave way beneath him, hurtling him down to the pavement at our feet.

Before any of us in the crowd could react, ambulance attendants lifted Charles's crumpled body onto a stretcher, and loaded him up for the trip to New Haven Hospital. Fourteen of us, who knew Charles well, followed the ambulance, literally running behind it until we reached the emergency room. We all crowded into the waiting room, desperately hoping that Charles would be all right, but each of us privately fearing that the injury was mortal. I knew Charles's family in Indianapolis, and tried to call them. I rang them repeatedly, but there was no answer.

The waiting room was crowded with us but oddly silent. Each of us was lost in his own thoughts. I wondered what had made him do such a dangerous, foolhardy, courageous thing. "What is it," I wondered, "that makes ordinary people do extraordinary things?" Courageous people always seemed to be distant figures, people set apart. I never expected to find a true hero among my friends. We were all ordinary people. Is each one of us a little bit hero and a little bit coward at the same time? Or is the hero one who truly believes that there is no real ending to life, just an ending for the body and a new beginning for the soul? Is the hero one who truly believes what all the great religions teach—'believe and you will be saved?' And if there is no death, but everlasting life, how can it matter whether our souls return to their source after a short life or a long one?

I was thinking these thoughts while standing and waiting, then I began to review the events of the night. I remembered Nathan Hale, his statue proud along the green. He, too, was an ordinary man who did extraordinary things for others, when he could have simply saved himself. I knew Charles would never be a national hero in history books or statues, but I knew he would never be forgotten by his friends or by the people he saved. He would always be remembered by the families of those he rescued and by everyone who watched his heroic acts. I was so wrapped up in these thoughts that I failed to notice when the doctor entered the room. I only saw him when he spoke, asking, "Are any of you family of Charles Sterling?"

I spoke up, "Charles is from Indianapolis. I tried calling his family, but no one answered the phone."

"I see," the doctor replied. "Well, would any of you like to come and see him?" All of us moved to follow him, but he said, "Wait a minute. You can't do this! All of you will not fit into his room." His comment deterred none of us, and, in the face of our determination, he gave in. "Oh, what's the difference? Come along." Then, he led us to the room.

The nurse left as we crowded in. The doctor checked Charles's pulse and then he left, too. We tried to stay back against the walls where we would not be in the way, but it was a very small room. With all the bodies crowded in, the heat was stifling, but we were happy to see that Charles looked so peaceful lying there. Despite his horrible ordeal, there was not a mark on his face. The doctor had not told us what to expect, but we all knew Charles's condition was very serious.

Just when I thought I could not bear the silence any more, Charles opened his eyes. He looked slowly at each of us in turn, as if trying to memorize our faces. I remember his smile had an almost blinding brightness that I had never seen before. He spoke softly, saying, "Don't feel sorry for me. Most people go through their whole lives and never get an opportunity like I had." Then, he closed his eyes and his smile faded. All the light seemed to leave his face. His breathing stopped, and we knew he was gone. We each bade him a silent farewell and filed out of the room.

None of us went untouched by that evening's events, and every October without fail, the fourteen of us gather together. We reflect on that night's events and pay our tribute to Charles, remembering, "Greater love hath no man than this, that a man lay down his life for his friends" (John 15: 13).

Louise Jones

Prom night was the biggest event of the year at Yale. The fellows dressed in tuxedos and bought lovely corsages for their dates. The girls were mostly students of the "Seven Sisters," as the famous women's colleges were called. They all tried to outdo each other with beautiful gowns and fancy hairstyles. The band was always a famous one—the year of my junior prom it was Rudy Vallee's.

All of us switched partners many times that night, as was the style then. At one point I was dancing with Jack Caldwell's fiancee, Barbara Ones. As we whirled around the floor, Barbara told me that she was giving a party that summer at her home in Lexington, Kentucky, and asked if I would attend. I said, "Of course, I would love to come." I thought it would add some excitement to the summer, and even if not, Jack was one of my best friends and my benefactor, so I couldn't refuse.

"Fine," Barbara replied, "It will be a big party and a nice weekend. I'll get a date for you." At that point, Jack cut in and I set out in search of another partner. I was having so much fun that I quickly forgot about Barbara and her party. Soon after prom, the year ended and I returned home to Springfield. Jobs were scarce at home because of the Great Depression, as it came to be known. So, I spent most of my time having fun with my friends and enjoying a life of relative leisure. Thoughts of Yale and commitments were far from my mind. With graduation coming the following spring, I knew this would likely be my last free summer.

One evening, when I returned home, I was greeted by my mother: "Son, there is a letter for you, from a Barbara Ones."

I opened it and found a formal invitation to Barbara's party in July. I had thought no more about it after prom, but now, suddenly, I remembered my promise. I explained the invitation and promise to my mother. She thought it was a long way for me to go alone, but, since she always loved Lexington and its huge horse farms, she offered to accompany me. I thought it was a wonderful idea and immediately wrote a letter to Barbara telling her that we were coming. I told her that since Mother was accompanying me, we would stay at a hotel so that she needn't worry about entertaining Mother for the weekend.

I knew several people had been invited to the party, and I figured I had to let her know politely that we would not be imposing on her hospitality. Barbara was a very nice girl, but I figured she probably lived on a small farm and that, while she would do her best, room for her guests would likely be at a premium. I knew Jack's penchant for rescuing the poor and downtrodden and prepared Mother for a small farm. We were quite surprised, on checking into the hotel, to find that the Ones's farm was one of the very large Bluegrass horse farms that my mother adored. It was huge, complete with a white mansion and a high white fence surrounding the grounds.

Barbara had arranged a small dinner party on Friday for the older guests, which my mother attended. The big party was scheduled to begin with a Tea Dance on Saturday afternoon at 5:00. My arranged date was a family friend of Barbara's, and, like most blind dates, she was nothing memorable or exciting. She was only seventeen and had little to interest a twenty-four-year-old college senior. But the object of the party was to have fun and to dance with as many people as possible, so both my date and I found more interesting partners elsewhere and had a wonderful time.

While I was dancing with Barbara, she asked, "Do you have to go back to the hotel tonight?"

"No," I replied.

"Well, after you take your date home, why don't you come back here? Jack is staying and you can room with him. We'll have breakfast together and continue the party."

"I'll do that," I said. "After I take my date home, I'll stop at the hotel to tell my Mother where I will be. Then I'll come back here."

It didn't take me long to drive the ten miles back to

Lexington and say goodnight to my date. Mother was asleep when I returned to the hotel, but I awakened her and told her about the party and Barbara's invitation. She told me that she didn't mind my returning to the Ones's, and so I headed back toward Barbara's house.

The house was set back from the road down a lane. There was a gate on the lane with a little lever that you pulled to gain access. When I made it down the lane to the house, all the lights were out. I thought I had not been gone long enough for the house to be closed. When I left, the party was in full swing; the band was still playing. Now, there were no cars, no people, no sign of servants cleaning up; it looked as if there had never been a party. I began talking to myself, trying to reason this out. "I know this is the right house. There's the upstairs room that Barbara showed me, the one I would be sharing with Jack. I began to mentally review the evening as I walked all the way around the house, looking for a light or an opened door to show that I was expected. There was neither.

I continued reasoning to myself, "It is only eight or ten miles back to Lexington. I took the girl home, we only chatted for a moment. I went to the hotel and only talked to Mother for a short while." By this time I had made it back to the front of the house and was standing under the window of the room I was to share with Jack. "Then, I came straight here."

I couldn't figure it out. When I left, the orchestra, a string ensemble, was playing a waltz and nobody showed any sign of leaving. The rugs were still rolled up and the furniture was still shoved against the wall to make room for dancing. Refreshments were still being served. All of those things would take time to put away. Even if most of the guests left when I did, there should still be somebody up, and some lights should be on.

I wondered if I should ring the bell, but decided that, since the balcony doors to the upstairs bedroom were open, I had probably just been gone longer than I realized. I decided to climb the trellis and let myself in, then I would ask Jack what happened. I climbed up, hopped over the iron balustrade, and walked right in the French doors—but the person in the bed was not Jack. The moonlight streaming in from the balcony revealed a beautiful woman, a blonde I had never seen before.

"Don't scream, Ma'am," I said quickly as she started up, clutching the sheet. "I think I've made a mistake."

"I think you have," she replied with remarkable composure.

"I could have sworn this was the Ones's house. I just left a party there and I was invited to come back and stay the night with my friend Jack. I thought the party must have just ended early, so I was going to let myself in."

"You're not the only one who has arrived at the wrong house," the girl laughed. "Although, the others came to the front door. The Oneses live on the next lane over. My grandfather and Barbara's grandfather were brothers and built identical houses."

"Why were you not at the party?" I asked. I was much more relaxed now since the girl was at ease and showed no signs of screaming for help. All the same, though, I went no farther into the room, staying near the window in case she changed her mind.

She hesitated before answering me, "I had a previous

engagement." Then she added, "You know, you don't have to go back down the trellis. You might fall. Why don't you just go through the room, down the front stairs and out the door?"

That was a sensible suggestion, and I headed for the hall door. But, before I reached it, I remembered a story I had read in high school about a Kentucky colonel who shot first and asked questions later. I hesitated and decided to return to the balcony.

"I think I had better go out the way I came up," I said.

"Suit yourself."

I headed out the doors, over the balustrade, and was partway down the trellis before I realized that I did not know who this lovely girl was. I climbed back up, and, poking my head back through the doors, I said, "I would like to meet you. What is your name?"

"Louise Jones."

"Miss Jones, I'm Howard Mumma. Could we have a date tomorrow? I'm from Ohio and will only be here this weekend."

"Why sure," she replied. "Why don't you and Barb come over for breakfast tomorrow, about ten."

"We'll be there." I was delighted. I climbed back down and hopped in the car. I arrived at the next lane and pulled an identical chain on an identical gate and drove to an identical house, except this one was lighted. I glanced in the window. Everything was as I left it, although the crowd was beginning to thin some. I walked in and immediately cut in on Barbara and we began dancing.

"Say," I asked casually, "who's the doll next door?"

Her reaction was all I had hoped for—she stopped in

mid step and stared at me in astonishment. "Where have you been?"

Gleeful inside, I remained casual, replying, "Where have I been? Well, you and I have a date for breakfast tomorrow at ten."

Barbara started dancing again. "Well, tell me now. How did you meet my cousin?"

"I'm an Ohio boy, I get around." I replied mysteriously.

I could tell Barbara was thinking furiously, but she simply said, "All right." We said nothing more about her cousin, but I chuckled to myself thinking how she might react if she knew how I met her cousin.

The party started to break up, and Jack and I said our good nights and headed to our room to get some sleep. Next morning, I awoke early and got ready to go. I ran into the maid and asked, "Where's Barb's room?" She pointed out the door, and, feeling quite devilish, I went over and banged on the door.

"Come on," I said. "We're going for breakfast."

To my surprise, Barbara came right out and we drove down to the Jones's. I got out and pulled open the gate. When I got back in the car, Barbara put her hand on my arm and said, "Now, stop for a moment. I'm not sure if you know this, but Louise can't walk."

At that point, I was sort of tumbling into love and beginning to make plans for our future together. Barb had stopped me dead. "What do you mean, she can't walk?"

"She is paralyzed from the hips down, from polio."

The news flattened me. In those days, polio was nearly always a death sentence and certainly precluded plans for marriage. No facilities for care and maintenance of those afflicted existed at that time, and the survivors became a tremendous financial burden that only the very rich could afford. I remembered Louise's hesitation when I asked her why she was not at the dance. I was ashamed to have caused her distress through my ignorance. I was numb as I continued down the lane. Louise was already seated at a table on the lawn when we arrived. A servant stood nearby, attending to her.

"Hello, Louise," said Barb, walking up and kissing her on the forehead. "I realize that the two of you have apparently met, but I would like to introduce you to Jack's friend Howard Mumma."

Barbara and I took seats at the table, and breakfast was served. It was a beautiful, sunny day, and the meal was superb. Once I regained my composure, we made pleasant conversation on a variety of topics. I don't remember what was said, but I do remember being very impressed by Louise—by her knowledge, her spirit, and her joy. The entire time that we spoke, I thought how much I liked and admired this lovely lady and how hopeless was my chance of having a closer relationship with her. I asked her permission to write and asked if she would write me. We agreed to start a correspondence.

"You know," Barb commented when we were back in the car, "a lot of fellows in Lexington would like to date Louise."

"I can understand that," I said, thinking of what good company Louise was and how much I had enjoyed the visit.

Barb went on, "But her father won't hear of it."

I could understand that, too. Only a very wealthy person could afford the servants and care that Louise would need for the rest of her life. I, unfortunately, knew I would never be that wealthy.

A few weeks later, I had a letter from Louise. It was as engaging and interesting as she, and I could picture her lovely face as I read it. I wrote back and we kept up our correspondence for several years. Although we never got serious, we were friends and remained very fond of each other. Louise died young, not too long after I graduated. I never went back to Lexington, but I never forgot the time, the place, and the beauty that was Louise.

The Beggar

A cold and dreary wind blew fitfully at my back. I was walking up Prospect Street Hill in New Haven. As I approached a streetlight, a decrepit old man stepped out of the shadows. He stopped me in the circle of light holding out his dirty hand, red with cold. He begged me to help him. Poverty had horribly ravaged this unhappy being—his eyes were swollen and runny, his clothes ragged, and he was covered in filthy sores.

Not only was I nauseated by the sight and scent of him, but I was frightened as well. The street was deserted. If he were armed and dangerous, no one could help. I rummaged through my pockets, but I had left my room with nothing—neither coin nor key, not even a handkerchief to offer. Still, he waited, watching me, holding out his hand.

I had nothing to give him, but I had an overpowering urge to give him something. A small voice inside told me that I did have something to give.

What could it be? I tried to put myself in his place. How would life be as a beggar? I tried to be objective. I saw the beggar with hand outstretched, stopping people on the street, asking for help. Some gave him money; some did not. But everyone hurried away from him as fast as they could, as if his poverty were a disease that they might catch. Most didn't want to see him; certainly, no one wanted to touch him.

"Touch!" I thought. "Warmth, friendliness—anyone can give him money, but no one stops to give him dignity. No one is concerned with his humanity. Money can solve an immediate need but cannot restore his battered soul." Sure of my course, I seized the beggar's dirty, trembling hand and shook it heartily. He stared at me in bewilderment and confusion.

"I'm sorry, brother, but I have nothing else to give you."

The beggar fixed his swollen eyes on mine, and they seemed to soften. He pressed my cold fingers in his, and I knew he understood. He said, "I know you have nothing material to give, but when all the others were afraid to touch me, you gave me your hand. You gave of yourself and called me 'Brother.' Thank you for that."

We parted. As I watched him walk away, I realized he had also given to me, and I remembered Christ's words, "Whatsoever you do unto the least of these, you also do unto me." I was grateful that I would no longer have to retreat in shame. The gospel had come alive for me.

Dr. Norman Vincent Peale

Nobody ever forgets his first real job, the one he's trained to do, the official one. I was trained to be a minister, a pastor, at Yale Divinity School. I studied the discipline of the United Methodist Church but felt like I didn't know much about being a pastor. Fortunately, my life to that point had prepared me better than I realized—for a parish is merely an association of individual people. A pastor can be of no aid to individuals during the one-hour Sunday service, but his work at all other times is very much one-on-one; kindness speaks a universal language.

In any event, I was surprised and delighted to be offered positions in both the Springfield and Columbus areas, during April of 1939, just before I graduated. The district superintendent in Columbus offered a choice of assistant minister at the university church or director of the Wesley Foundation. The district superintendent in Springfield offered a "two-point circuit," whatever that was.

To help in making a wise choice, I called on a man I had recently read about and whom I admired, Dr. Norman Vincent Peale. I thought he would be able to help because he had once been a pastor in Ohio himself, and his father once served as pastor of the First Methodist Church in Columbus—obviously he would know all the answers. When I called his telephone number, a secretary gave me an appointment for Monday morning. I took the train to New York City on Sunday and stayed the night at the YMCA.

Dr. Peale received me graciously at 10:00 Monday morning, saying that he had not thought about Methodism in Ohio for many years. I told him that I knew both he and his father had been ministers in the state, and that is why I had come to him. He read the two letters I had received, laughed and said, "I know the minister at the university quite well. I know the director of the Wesley Foundation. I also know Magnetic Springs and Pharisburg; they are about twenty miles west of Delaware, Ohio. Young man, do you know anything about living in the country?"

"I spent a summer on a farm once, but I don't know anything about church life there or about farms."

"My advice to you is to accept the two-point circuit and work with the farmers. If you have anything, you will get an appointment soon enough in the city. If you do not have anything to offer, you may spend your ministry in the rural community and still be richly rewarded."

I followed Dr. Peale's advice, and he was right. My two

years in a rural ministry proved to be the richest experience of my life. I learned to love the farmers and they
learned to love me.

The Robinsons and
Aunt Martha

June was a busy time for me. First there was graduation. Then I made the trip to Columbus to be tested by the Committee on Ordination and ordained. I was surprised to be presented by the committee with only two questions, each on its own sheet of paper, requiring only my signature in response. The first asked me to promise I would never use alcohol or tobacco in any form. I had no difficulty with that. My father had promised his three sons their choice, at age 21, of either one hundred dollars or a gold watch if we neither drank alcohol, nor smoked. My eldest brother took the money. I took the gold watch and have always kept it with me. The middle brother, however, had been a star athlete and had accompanied his teammates to a beer celebration hosted by a triumphant coach, thereby disqualifying himself.

The second paper I was asked to sign made me promise never to become indebted to the extent that I would embarrass the church. I confessed to some debts left over from college years, but they were more concerned about a minister leaving town without paying his grocery bills. When I expressed wonder that they had not questioned my theology, they said they merely assumed that my beliefs were acceptable, and were more interested in my ethics and morals. The committee chairman had one last request: "Promise me that you will never take the arm of a woman parishioner to help her up the steps, until she has passed her seventieth birthday!"

Also, when the bishop found out that I had not graduated from a college or divinity school of my chosen denomination, he said, "I want that young man to have a three-year trial period instead of two!" That meant that I would be carefully watched for three years, but, in truth, all ministers are carefully watched for at least forty.

When the appointment list was read on the last day of the Ohio Annual Conference, I was proud to hear my name and my appointment to the churches of Magnetic Springs and Pharisburg—really, my first church would be two churches. The District Superintendent informed me that my salary would be $1200, $600 from each church, and a parsonage in Magnetic Springs.

My mother and I drove to Magnetic Springs three days later. We found the parsonage, a five-room house with a living room, a study, a kitchen, a bathroom, and two upstairs bedrooms. The kitchen contained a stove and a refrigerator, both examined and pronounced satisfactory by my mother, and a linoleum floor. The living room had a worn carpet, and the bedroom floors were bare. We sat on the floor and made a shopping list.

Before returning home, we took a ride through the area to look at the two villages that comprised my circuit. They were only three miles apart but different as day and night. Pharisburg was an unincorporated village surrounded by farms. It had the shared elementary school, a small church, and a general store, but no parsonage or hotel. Magnetic Springs drew its name from the healing waters that attracted people from miles around. They came in the "season"—spring, summer, and fall—for relief from arthritis, problems with alcohol, and other symptoms and syndromes. The winter population of about 200 swelled to 800 in season. The guests were accommodated in the three local hotels built by enterprising landowners. The larger church, high school, junior high school, and meeting rooms were all in this village.

Mother and I took our list and bought the furniture I would need—a sofa, two armchairs, a desk and chair, a table with four chairs, and a bed. We hired a trucker to deliver it, and, in two days, we were unloading the furniture at my new home. Two ladies came to greet us and Mother arranged regular cleaning of my house with one of them who lived nearby. The other, Mrs. Conrad, then introduced herself and asked Mother about my cooking. "Howard can't cook," she said, "but I am sure he can learn and then eat out once in a while."

Mrs. Conrad, however, had a better idea, "The Doctor Conrad Hotel is only a block away from here. If the

Reverend would like, he can have three meals a day for just one dollar."

Mother was thrilled: "That's wonderful! That's just what Howard will do!" I felt superfluous since Mother and my new neighbors were busy planning my life, so I went for a walk. After exploring a bit, I returned to the parsonage and took Mother to Dr. Conrad's before driving her home. When we were seated, I asked the waitress for a glass of water, and she looked surprised. Shortly after, Dr. Conrad came to our table and introduced himself, saying, "Reverend, you should never drink water during the hour before a meal or the hour after. It dilutes the digestive juices."

The doctor's hotel accommodated 35 to 40 guests who listened to his Wednesday evening lectures and followed his rules for health. Each of them was in bed by 9:30 each evening, and, over the course of the night, drank a half-gallon jug of Magnetic Springs water, if they wanted breakfast. With this treatment, it was no surprise they got well.

On my first Sunday, I conducted my services at 9:00 in Magnetic Springs and at 10:30 in Pharisburg. After each service, I stood at the door to greet the parishioners. A woman told me that her father was ill and asked if I would call on him. That afternoon, I followed her directions, and, several miles out of town, made my first pastoral call. That was a shocker! The woman took me upstairs where her father sat in bed smoking a big cigar. He welcomed me to town, and said he hoped I would be happy there. He had had a hard life working in a factory and was now 86 years old. I asked him to what he attributed his long life, and, leaning over, he reached under his bed and pulled out a pint bottle of whiskey, half full. He held the bottle in one hand and the cigar in the other. "These are the two things that gave me a long life." After a pleasant visit, I excused myself. When I got home, I said to myself, "Howard, you are out of academia and living in a world with real people."

I was the only minister serving this ten-square-mile area with its two churches, so I started making house calls. I simply knocked on doors and introduced myself, inviting the people to church. Soon, I began to get invitations to meals—lunch as well as dinner. I wanted to get to know the community, so I accepted every invitation. I ended up opening PTA meetings, giving opening prayers at lodges, Farm Bureau meetings, and 4-H gatherings. Within four or five months, I knew every family in my circuit, and that's how it should be.

Young, married farmers have a variety of tricks to play on a newcomer. One church group had 25 couples that met the first Sunday of every month to enjoy potluck suppers. Everybody brought something to share, and supper was followed by games. (I grew up real fast in response to their games.) For one of their favorites, we all sat on the floor in a big circle. Two men were picked to lie in the middle of the circle with sheets over them. Somebody from the circle would swat one of them with a yardstick, and the swatted one would grab off his sheet and try to grab the swatter. After one or two turns, I was selected by the group to be the swatter. My instructions were to swat, and then quickly hand the stick to my neighbor. I was not fast enough and got caught. Now it was my turn to get on the floor and cover my head. My leg took a hard blow, but when I ripped off the sheet, everyone showed me empty hands. After two or three licks, I found out it was the man beside me on the floor! He had the stick hidden under his sheet.

Later I wanted to make a hit with the farmers, so I went one day to what they called a combine. Six or eight farmers and their wives would combine to harvest the oats, peas, and barley. They would haul the crop into the barn and pitch it up to a man in the loft who would fork it into stacks. They put me in the loft (I think it was a sort of initiation) where the temperature must have climbed to 115°F. There were four farmers in the barn throwing, but I was alone in the loft. After two hours, I was dead on my feet. I climbed back down the ladder and the five of us exited the barn and joined the harvesters in the house for a huge dinner. They invited me to work some more after dinner, but I uttered my first prevarication. I told them I had pastoral calls to make. In reality, I went home and took a four-hour nap.

In any event, I settled into a daily routine. I rose at 6:30 to have a bountiful breakfast at Dr. Conrad's Hotel and visit with the guests. Then I came home for morning prayers, read and worked on sermons until noon. After a light lunch, I would set off to make pastoral calls, systematically so that no one would be missed. At 6:00 I went to dinner and usually a meeting somewhere. I was always home by 9:30. On my afternoon visits, I never visited any family very often, so as not to wear out my welcome. No family, that is, except the Robinsons.

Walter and Elsa Robinson gave me my best taste of life in a farm family. They had four sons in school. I enjoyed meals there at least once a month, and, no matter where my calls took me, I always made sure to get to the Robinson's house Thursday at 3:30. I went first into the barn to say hello to Walter, then to the kitchen. There, Elsa would be taking fresh-baked bread out of the oven. She always happened to have an extra loaf for me. I ate some of that bread every night before bed with a glass of milk. Nothing else before or since ever tasted that good. The Robinson family won a place in my heart.

Every time I visited a home, someone there would ask if I had visited Aunt Martha yet. Eventually, I walked to the house where she lived and knocked on the door. A nurse in uniform answered. I told her that I was the new minister and hoped to meet Aunt Martha. She picked up a piece of paper from the hall table and reported that my name was not on today's list.

"Do I have to have an appointment to see Aunt Martha," I asked, incredulous.

"Do you know Aunt Martha?"

"No, I only know that she lives here."

"Many people come to see Aunt Martha, and she can only see four or five people a day. I can give you a half-hour on the 13th at 2:00." Curious, I promised to be on time.

When I began questioning residents about her, I learned that she was well known and treasured in many states. She had inspired the Governor of Ohio, several U.S. Senators, a Supreme Court Justice and even presidents and executives of corporations. Prominent people from many cities made appointments to see her—an invalid in a tiny village. I became anxious to meet her, so at the appointed time, I knocked on her door. A man came to greet me and said that Aunt Martha was looking forward to my visit. In a bedroom off the back of the living room, a beautiful woman sat in bed with both hands outstretched to me. "Young man, I have been looking forward to this moment."

I looked up into her beautiful, blue eyes and felt like I was in the presence of a saint. I found myself on my knees beside her bed. She laid her hands on me and prayed that God would bless me and my ministry. I rose with tears in my eyes, as she said, "I will pray for you each day and ask God to make you a true minister of the Lord Jesus Christ."

As the nurse and the secretary escorted me to the door, I was walking on a cloud, wondering how an 80-year-old woman could be so beautiful, so powerful, so inspiring. During my sojourn in rural Ohio, I was fortunate enough to be able to see her several more times for her blessing.

The Children of Ohio

Four years of college and three in Yale Divinity School had not prepared me for my responsibilities in these two little churches. I called on my imagination and relied heavily on trial and error. With less than two weeks on the job, I learned that one of my responsibilities was to teach Vacation Bible School. I was given about 15 fourth- and fifth-graders for two weeks. I had no guidelines and no idea how to approach them or what to do first. So, I asked them what they should be doing. They had several suggestions—one was to go swimming. Another was to take a hike. The third was to tell them Bible stories.

I told my class that the next day I would tell them the story of Shadrach, Meshach, and Abednego. They had never heard it. Eighteen young people showed up to hear the story of the three friends of Daniel who survived the fiery furnace. Then, when I told them the story of Daniel in the den of lions, I got the idea to have them act out the story. Everybody had a part, not only the four heroes, but also the kings and all the lions. We did not worry about costuming, but had a lot of fun acting. I would read a few lines and the children would act. We spent the second week doing different stories from both the Old and New Testaments—Moses as a baby, found among the reeds; Abraham and Isaac; Jacob deceiving his father; even Stephen being stoned for his faith. We started a tradition in that church that went on for 10 or 15 years—the pastor developing stories and the young people acting. I never felt quite sure about what we were doing, but we all had a good time. On the last day of Bible School, the children asked, "Why can't we go on? Why not do this every day?"

It was time for a counter question: "Would you like to form a choir and learn to sing?" Everyone agreed that it was a good idea and wanted me to direct. I confessed I was unable to lead the choir but promised to get them a director. I called a group of mothers to meet and talk about a choir. They approved. We had a party with cake and ice cream; then we organized the choir. One of the mothers had had some training in music and agreed to direct. After a few rehearsals, I came in to listen to them. I announced, "These children ought to have robes—black robes with white surplices." That idea quickly caught on, and about forty women came in to sew robes.

Then we were ready for their first performance. The news was printed in the paper that the children's choir would sing on the first Sunday of every month. They came

in early and put on their new robes. It was a glorious performance that first Sunday, one of the finest I ever had.
Everyone was pleased. About two months later, however,
came a Sunday of great embarrassment to me—it was a
long time before I learned to laugh about it. The children's
choir director announced that they were ready to sing a
very fine anthem that would fit well with Holy
Communion and wondered if I would let them sing on that
Sunday. I agreed but began thinking about the children having to either leave the church after singing or sit in the corner and watch while their parents received the elements.

The week before Holy Communion was scheduled, I
told the children about the meaning of the Last Supper. I
brought in the bread and the grape juice and showed them
how to come to the altar and take the bread from me and
eat it and then take the juice and drink it all the while thinking about Jesus dying on the cross for the forgiveness of the
sins of the world. (At least, I tried my best to explain the
significance of Communion.) After the anthem, the children
came to the altar, and I explained to the parents that the
children would receive Holy Communion. The parents
took pictures as I gave each child the bread, and they held
out their hands for the tiny glass of juice. I had started at
one end of the line then stopped because I heard a hiccup.
I ignored it, but I heard another. When I had served all of
them, all of the 32 children were hiccuping out of control!
Nothing since has ever been so embarrassing.

At the next official board meeting, I felt it proper to
apologize for the outbreak. I explained my lack of previous experience with children. I said I thought that the children's choir and Vacation Bible School were most benefi-

cial to the church, but that giving the children Communion had been a mistake, and I was sorry. To my astonishment, first one, then another, and another of the older members rose to say, "Sir, it was no mistake. You did what you felt was right, and we hope you continue to let the children take Communion and help them to thus continue to grow in Christian life."

The church officials believed that it was appropriate for the children to sing in church once or twice a month and to continue to take Communion. The story even got into the papers and drew a call from my District Superintendent. He merely suggested that I might consult with the parents of the children in the choir to see if there could be a change made in their breakfast menus for the days that they would be taking Communion.

The School Board

In my two years on my 2-point circuit, I learned many things about human nature, people, and politics. The leaders in the churches were also the leaders of the schools, the lodges, and the town council. Anything that went on in one group fell under the same watchful eyes as the others. The public school superintendent was also the director of the Sunday school. He asked me to sit in on a school board meeting while they interviewed two prospective teachers. Most teachers who applied to work there were graduates of Ohio State University. They were unable to get jobs in the city because they lacked experience, so they were forced to work in the rural areas. They would work for the small school systems only until better opportunities arose. Of course, the turnover was high; few teachers would stay where salaries were small and advancement virtually impossible.

I listened while the second prospect was interviewed. The salary was set and the contract about to be signed when the school board chairman said, "Now, Mr. B., we come to the final matter before you sign. We have a little rule here that states that all teachers will agree to be in church on Sunday morning and will teach Sunday school if asked."

Mr. B. replied, "I do not belong to any church and have no intention of going to church."

"I'm sorry, but we cannot use you. We have no room for you here," was the only reply.

I did not sleep that night searching and praying for help to decide what action I should take. I later found that this practice was entrenched, having gone on for years. All my predecessors had agreed or, at least, raised no objection. In no way could I endorse this behavior or be silent. I spoke to the school board members individually, privately and publicly, trying my best to explain that the Constitution of the United States of America clearly stated, in the Bill of Rights, that church and state must remain separate.

My training for the ministry had not included examples that would help in such a case. Local customs and unwritten rules often operate outside the Constitution and the Bill of Rights. Nobody agreed with me that a good public school teacher was not necessarily going to be a good Sunday school teacher. Finally, I held my tongue. There comes a time in every ministry where you are forced to realize that you are not God.

Bud and Alice

Another difficult task for a new ministry is marital, or more often pre-marital, counseling. My first couple to counsel about marriage did not fit any example in the books I was reading or in the notes from the semester course at Yale Divinity. The professor had talked about types of problems we might meet, but this couple was a challenge. I originally thought that giving general advice and pamphlets would answer any questions Bud and Alice might present, but I was wrong. After the preliminaries, Bud said, "None of this is any help to us. We have a real problem. My family does not approve of Alice as a bride for me."

Alice was an attractive girl. She had grown up in an orphanage and had taken a job as Bud's grandmother's maid. Bud was a member of a prominent, prospering farming family. All of the family lived in the community and attended the church. They were very proud of their heritage. The widowed mother of seven sons and daughters wanted to remain in the family home, so her sons and daughters hired a well-recommended young woman, Alice, to be a companion and helper for the elderly, but still dominant grandmother.

When I made my first pastoral call, Alice served us lemonade and was asked to sit and meet the new pastor. At that time, no one knew that Bud and Alice had fallen in love. They wanted to be married and wanted to stop meeting in secret. Bud asked me to intercede for him in an attempt to make the family drop its opposition. I doubted that it was my place or that I could change anyone's mind. All the same, I did mention to the family that the couple wanted to do the right thing. I got a look that told me what they thought of my interference in their affairs.

Bud and Alice came to talk many times, thinking of all possible actions. Bud wanted to run away with Alice, but Alice thought that they should stop seeing each other. Eventually the family ran out of objections to Alice, who had maintained a pleasant demeanor through the entire affair. They finally welcomed her into the family, and I was allowed to perform the sacrament of marriage for my two dear friends.

I heard from Alice thirty-nine years later, when Bud died, asking me to come to the funeral. I was out of the country when the letter arrived, but I wrote her back as soon as I returned home. She told me they had had a wonderful life, and that she now had three sons and two daughters to comfort her.

It doesn't seem that long ago. My two years in Magnetic Springs flew by all too quickly. I had mixed emotions about my assignment to a different parish. Why? I had known nothing about rural life; I learned. I had known nothing about farmers—I learned to love my parishioners and think they came to love me. When my time at Magnetic Springs was up, the town gave me a farewell dinner. At the dinner, an old man, a revered leader, made a short speech. He said, "When Howard came to us, as a young, single pastor, we decided that we were going to watch him very carefully. It was not long, though, before we discovered that he was watching us."

The Yarings

After a few more years in the pulpit, I was assigned to a parish in Toledo, Ohio, but the most memorable experience of my time there proved to be an international one. The Council of Bishops of the Methodist Church appointed and accredited me to be a certified, official visitor to the First World Council of Churches, which was to be held in Amsterdam, Holland, in June of 1948. The letter containing the announcement was delivered by the same mailman that I saw nearly every day, but suddenly he appeared to be a heavenly messenger. What an honor!

The local newspaper heard about it and a week later the *Toledo Blade* sent a photographer over, and my picture appeared in the paper. The editor, Grove Patterson, was a friend. After the story ran, he called to invite me to lunch. It was a good lunch, but soon an ulterior motive appeared.

"Howard," he said, "here's a letter I got from the State Department. They ask if I would like to visit Warsaw and Prague, behind the Iron Curtain. It sounds interesting, but I know my health will not permit the trip. But you are going to Europe anyhow to be a delegate to the First World Council of Churches—I read that in the paper. If you could substitute for me after the meeting, it would be a once-in-a-lifetime experience for you. You are younger and friskier than I am, and you write well. I can arrange it all with the State Department, and you can tell me all about it when you get home."

"In the first place, I am not going to be a delegate, I will be an official visitor without voting or speaking rights. Secondly, things are pretty lively at home since our third daughter arrived, not to mention that, from what I've heard, life behind the Iron Curtain is unpredictable and dangerous."

"Sure, there is a little risk involved. Why don't you just triple your life insurance? You're a young fellow and you should be venturesome."

I asked my wife what I should do. She listened and said, "Whatever you want to do will be all right with me." I had to make the decision and live with the consequences. After a lot of thought and little sleep, I called Grove Patterson and told him that I would watch history in the making. My friend summarized, "Now remember, you have to pay your own way. I don't even know how much protection you will have. Our State Department has no power east of the Iron Curtain."

A member of the church asked me to call on a relative of his while I was in Amsterdam. I arrived there a week early not only for the scheduled visit, but also because I wanted to see as much as I could of the city. I did not know how much time I might have after the Council meetings. The family I was calling on in Amsterdam was named Yaring, Mr. and Mrs. Yaring Yaring, to be exact. (The first and last names were the same. They did not think it was strange so I tried not to let them think that I did either.) They told me about their experiences during the Nazi occupation. The first thing the German soldiers did when they occupied the area was snatch all the teenage boys they could find out of their homes and send them to Germany. They went, not to become soldiers, but to replace the workers in the factories. The Yarings were determined that their son, Jon, now 18, would not be taken.

The family went to extraordinary lengths to protect him from the Nazis. Mr. Yaring and Jon worked long and hard to dig a tunnel under their house, four feet deep and twelve feet wide. Fortunately, the Nazis announced their arrival by kicking in the doors of the houses they were going to search. When the Yarings heard the procession of kicked-in doors, Jon would have enough time to descend through a hole in the floor and lower himself into the tunnel. Jon sometimes spent up to 22 hours a day in the tunnel during the four years of occupation. The safest time for him to come out was between 2 and 4 AM. Then he could get washed, run around, and exercise. His sister, who was 14 at the time of the occupation, was sent off with other teenage girls, carefully chaperoned, to work on the farms. The parents told these stories with tears visible in their eyes.

I spent two days with the Yaring family, exchanging life stories as we learned more about each other's countries. Before I left, I asked if there were anything special they would like me to send them when I got back to Ohio. Mr. Yaring thought he would like a few copies of *National Geographic*; his wife and daughter said, "Nylons!" and added, "and maybe some nuts."

After I got home, Mrs. Mumma bought a dozen pairs of nylon stockings and mailed them in a box with assorted nuts. The U.S. Post Office asked what the package contained and wrote "Nylons" on the wrapping paper. We got thanks for the magazines and the nuts, but no mention of the nylons. So, my wife bought another dozen pair of nylons and wrapped them up with some clothing and stationery. She labeled the box "stationery." Soon there came a heartfelt thanks for the nylons!

During my time in Amsterdam, I also visited the house where Anne Frank lived and wrote her story of hiding from the Nazis. She and many others went through untold hardships during that bitter time, and for many it ended in death.

On a happier note, I found the masterworks of Dürer, Rubens, and Rembrandt in the wonderful Rijksmuseum, a consoling contrast to man's inhumanity. I also took part in the night celebration in which Queen Wilhelmina threw the switch that lighted all the canals again, for the first time since the war. It was thrilling to be a part of it and delightful to see the singing and laughing as so many people rejoiced together.

Finally, at the Council, more than a thousand delegates from all over Christendom assembled, opening the First

Council in affirmation of a "fellowship of churches which accept our Lord Jesus Christ as God and Savior." It was truly the beginning of ecumenism—seeking to be an instrument of church unity in faith and outlook. For months preceding the opening, anticipation was high that the Roman Catholic Church would be an official part of this council. Alas, at the last moment, barely 72 hours before the opening session, came the announcement that the Vatican had decided to withdraw from membership.

At least they permitted their already appointed delegates to become official, accredited visitors, without votes, but the decision still cast a pall over the first session. The Roman Catholic visitors were seated behind the boundary, in the same section as my seat. Even though I could not vote, it was a thrilling experience for me to see all the notable leaders on the platform: Queen Wilhelmina, the prime minister, the bishops of the Dutch Reformed Church, and all the other officials.

On an unofficial basis, I had some very rewarding experiences. The main speaker at the first session was Dr. Karl Barth, a leading theologian of the twentieth century and professor of theology at the University of Basel. It was a masterful address. A few days later, while I was eating breakfast he came and sat with me. He knew very little English, but we made ourselves understood and, for me, it was a high point.

During the three weeks of the conference, I came to know a number of my fellow ministers from England and Germany and decided to give a luncheon for ten of them, five from each country. Their countries had been enemies, but we shared a common experience as Methodist pastors.

They all accepted my invitation. The church in Toledo had given me a sum of money to help with my expenses, and I used it for a delicious luncheon in a private dining room at the hotel. I introduced everyone, and we sat at a long, narrow table. The British were on one side and the Germans on the other. The waiters explained the menu and we gave our orders. The Germans ordered beer, and the British were aghast! Then, after dessert, the British pastors all pulled out pipes, filled them, and puffed away. Now the Germans were shocked! In England, Methodists did not drink alcohol, did not go to the theater, and did not read the newspaper on Sunday. The Germans deeply disapproved of any minister using tobacco. While no one spoke a word of their feelings, I could tell them from their expressions. It was a wonderful meal, but I was glad when it was over.

Fritz Schaefer and
my Blessed Pilots

When the conference concluded, I took the train to Frankfurt, Germany, and reported to the military headquarters, as I had been instructed. The desk sergeant found my name in his book and said, "You are on the list. However, only two flights per week go in that direction. The next one goes out day after tomorrow. Be at the airport at 6:00 AM."

I found a hotel in downtown Frankfurt and spent my free day doing some sightseeing. Everywhere I saw the rubble and destruction left from the War. I returned to the airport at the appointed time only to find that my flight had been canceled. The sergeant, on his own authority, offered me a flight into Berlin on the "Airlift." (That was the American solution to the blockade of Berlin.) It seemed my only option, so I agreed. I got a ride to the runway where 10 or 12 planes were ready to go. I got into one of them with two young American pilots.

"Meet your fellow passengers," the captain laughed, pointing back to where the seats should have been. Instead of seats the belly of the plane was full of large bags of white flour. "Sit back there on the flour," he instructed.

Not too long after take off, some of the bags got loose, broke open, and spilled flour on everything, especially me. The pilots finally decided they had to let me sit in the cockpit, flour and all. (Perhaps they didn't like the idea of a ghost flying in the cargo compartment.) We landed at Templehof, a small airfield, not designed to handle the big planes of the Airlift. As an American civilian, I was directed to a special desk. The attendant, an attractive, young lady, asked if I had any requests.

I told her I would like to get in touch with the minister of a local parish. With her help, I found the number and called the minister, Fritz Schaefer. He was delighted to hear from me and came to the airport. After greeting me and introducing his wife, he said, "You are preaching here Sunday morning, and in the evening you are to be the guest speaker at the chapel in Air Templehof."

I traded my services for three days of hospitality and guided tours. I had a delightful time. Fritz interpreted my remarks for his German congregation because I found that my college German was Greek for my audience in Berlin. I also saw the start of reconstruction. We watched the changing of the guard as the American, British, French, and Russian officers took their turns in government over the divided city. The Schaefers bid me God-speed at Air

Templehof after the service; I had a flight at 7:30.

I got into an empty plane to fly to Wiesbaden. The route of the Airlift was down a narrow air corridor, all one way. Planes were taking off every three minutes. No sooner were we airborne than we were struck by lightning, which really rocked the airplane (worse even than it would have had the plane been full.) Our lights kicked out and the wireless was gone, meaning that we could not call Air Templehof for help.

"Let's turn back," said the copilot, but there was a long line of airplanes right behind us and the risk of collision was too great.

"We don't dare," returned the pilot, "we'll just have to trust to luck." We had neither running lights nor interior lights and so they asked me to join them in the cockpit.

I asked, "Is there anything I can do for you?"

"Pray!" they said in unison, and I did, for quite some time.

The young American pilots kept checking the time and we seemed to be flying too long. On routine trips, the Berlin–Wiesbaden leg was a short one. We had plenty of fuel, but we could no longer see familiar landmarks. To complicate matters, it was pitch dark.

The pilot finally said, "I'm lost." He was flying as low as he dared while we looked for lights, airfields, and cities. "I'm going down," he muttered, and then we saw the water!

"It's the English Channel!" Now I was scared. The pilot took us up again, checking the gasoline level by his cigarette lighter. Then we saw the lights of old *Le Bourget* field, where Lindbergh had landed, and we set down.

In the morning, we filled the tanks and had the electrical systems checked. We flew on to Wiesbaden, still with no running lights, by following landmarks. From there, I took the train to Frankfurt. My friendly sergeant's jaw dropped to see me. "Where have you been? The State Department sent a communique about you. They want to know if you got to Warsaw yet. I told the colonel 'No' and he cabled back that you are scheduled to go to Warsaw tomorrow."

The Ambassador in Warsaw and Archbishop Beran

After my sojourn in Berlin, I was not all that sure I wanted to go to Warsaw, but then I remembered I was supposed to be venturesome. At 7:00 AM, I boarded a Polish airplane, a utilitarian vehicle with hard, wooden benches fastened to the floor. The ride to Warsaw was beautiful, despite the accomodations—the sun was shining, the fields were fertile and orderly, and my thought was, "We are in God's world."

After we landed, we taxied toward the airport, and I immediately saw two men in military uniforms waiting on the tarmac. When the plane stopped and the door opened, they boarded. One of them said, in broken English, "We are looking for Reverend Mumma."

I deplaned with them and was escorted off to the left.

When I glanced around, I saw that all the other passengers were heading in the opposite direction, toward the main entrance. My escort took me off to a small room where I was forced to wait for an hour with no explanations. Finally, a handsome, elegantly uniformed Polish colonel joined me, saying, "Reverend Howard Elwood Mumma, born in Springfield, Ohio, 1909—we would like to ask you a few questions." I was amazed by the fact he spoke perfect English, unlike my earlier escort.

I saw no way to refuse and, still being venturesome, followed him to another room. This was smaller than the first, completely windowless, and lit by a single, powerfully bright ceiling fixture. Two soldiers were already in the room and directed me to sit beneath the light. With the light beating directly down on me, everyone else was in shadow. I was to be involved in a classic, spy movie interrogation. For 72 hours I only left my seat when I was escorted to the bathroom. The colonel began the questions that would go on and on. For 72 hours, they were always the same questions: "Tell me about Springfield, Ohio. What is the first thing you remember as a little boy growing up there? Who were your playmates? What were their names? I want the names of each of your friends while you were growing up."

He questioned me continuously for four hours. When he stopped, another officer came in and repeated the same questions. Then, they let me nap for 15 minutes and started over. A few times they brought me sandwiches and a cider-like beverage. I didn't care for the drink, so they brought me vodka instead. Like all vodka, it smelled like turpentine, and I settled for water.

The questions kept coming, questions about my religion, my politics, and even my social life. They traced my life from childhood until I moved to Toledo. They asked about Grove Patterson and the *Toledo Blade*. Nobody gave a hint of what they were after. I didn't know what they wanted of me. I was getting more tired and cross. It was all unreasonable.

Then the colonel came back in with a sheaf of papers. He read me what was on them, the questions and my answers, then he said, "I am happy to tell you that you have answered all my questions truthfully. . . ." I was disgusted—of course I had. Angered, I asked some questions of my own: "Where did you learn to speak English so well? And why did you bring me here?!"

"When we found out you were substituting for Mr. Patterson, we had to find out more about you and if you were sent for some purpose. When we found out that you were just a dumb, American clergyman, we were willing to receive you." He smiled for the first time and named the American university he had attended for two years. "Then I went to Moscow for more training. I am now number three in the Polish Army."

Then, finally, they let me go. Happily, I never saw any of them again. The American ambassador and his aide were waiting for me in the same area that I had occupied while waiting to be interrogated. The aide said, "You were in there for 72 hours. They kept telling us, 'Just a few more hours and we'll release him.' We could do nothing but wait. We have been here, in shifts with the rest of the staff, for three days."

Being weak and tired from my ordeal, I rested at the

embassy for a few days. Before that adventure, I would not have believed what I did when I returned to American soil. As soon as I arrived at the embassy, I fell to my knees and kissed the ground, thanking God for my country's freedom. After I recovered from the trial of entering Poland, I was invited to the summer palace of the Roman Catholic Archbishop, Joseph Beran, who was responsible for both Poland and Czechoslovakia. If I had received that invitation in Ohio, I would have accepted without question, but here I was, understandably, a bit anxious outside the embassy walls. The ambassador was out of town so I asked his attaché if he thought I should accept.

"I don't know the Archbishop, I'm not Catholic."

"Well, neither am I," I replied, laughing at how absurd this would sound in Toledo.

"If you wish to accept the invitation, we will see that you get there and back in an embassy car."

Again, I reminded myself that I was supposed to be venturesome, so I accepted the invitation. I was driven out into the country to a big farmhouse that turned out to be the "summer palace." I was surprised when the archbishop answered his own door. He was a small man dressed as a simple priest. Crowding behind him were four people I took to be housekeepers and farmhands.

"Welcome!" he said warmly, and continued in understandable, but broken English: "Before we visit, could we pray together?" And right there in the hallway, we knelt. First he prayed and then I prayed. No priest before or after that ever asked for my prayers. I was deeply moved. We went from the hall into his study where I learned that he thought I was a diplomat from America. I told him the story of how I came to be in Warsaw and that I was also to visit Prague, where I would be staying with Dr. Joseph Hromadka. He gave me the name of a priest whom he would like me to meet and told me his own story. I came to find out that he had been put under house arrest for five years by the Polish government. I was less than thrilled to be in the company of a known dissident and was very happy when I was safely back at the embassy.

The People Behind the Wall

I was taken from the embassy on a tour of the Jewish Ghetto of Warsaw, where many of Poland's Jews had been confined during the war. When Hitler ordered the ghetto destroyed, a quarter of a million people were herded together so that the air force could dump petrol over them and set it and them afire. After the fire had run its course, men drove bulldozers in and covered the remains with dirt. This mass murder had happened here in 1944. On a warm August day in 1948, as I walked over the area, I was nearly overcome by the terrible stench of burnt flesh.

On the tour, I was again mistaken for an American diplomat, and was invited, by a stranger, to visit the Polish underground. Not sure what to say, I again asked the attaché's opinion. His cheery answer was, "We have no responsibility for you there. If you lose your life or are arrested, we can do nothing to help."

At the time, the situation made me very anxious, but in hindsight I wouldn't have missed that adventure for the world. An American lieutenant and a sergeant volunteered to go with me, and the embassy was kind enough to furnish a Jeep for the trip. The next night at 11:00, we rode out into the quiet streets with our lights out. We headed out into the country, and for hours, after we left the highway, we drove into the darkness. Several times we were stopped and inspected by flashlight, but we were let go. Finally a group of men stopped us and led us to an abandoned schoolhouse. We were led around back where we came upon two doors flat on the ground, surrounded by tall weeds. We were led down the stairs and then we crawled through a tunnel. I was excruciatingly claustrophobic, but just as it became unbearable, I sensed that we were in a new darkness, one occupied by many people. Finally two lighted candles appeared on a long table around which about 200 people were gathered—some sitting, some standing. They paid no attention to us, knowing by this time that we were official visitors from America. The lieutenant translated their remarks for me and mine for them.

The leader of the meeting was a strong man with a forceful presence. He asked me to say a few words since I, too, was a leader—as an American pastor of a city church. I spoke to them about the freedom we enjoy in America: freedom of thought, of assembly, of worship, of expression. I told them I hoped that they would never stop trying to gain such freedom for their country. Yet, I realized that their suffering and hardship would continue into the foreseeable future. I wanted so badly to bestow an act of kindness, to help even one of them, but it was not in my power to do so that night.

They closed their meeting with songs of support for each other in the fight against communism, as well as folk songs they had sung as children. They were aware that their lives were in danger. At any time, they could have been sealed off where they were. They had little food and little hope, but the songs helped to cement their friendship and purpose. Several people came up to greet me, but only one of them spoke English, an old man with white hair and beard.

"Thank you for coming. I am a professor at Warsaw University." His eyes filled with tears as he said, "May I ask you about America? Is it true that you can travel from one coast to another, all over the country, without a government pass? Is it true that you may criticize the President and remain free? Is it true that everyone in America has a suit of clothes or a dress and a pair of shoes, too?

"Yes, I think almost everybody does."

Then he started to cry. He took me by the lapels, and his hands began to shake. "Oh, if I only could live long enough to see that kind of life in Poland!"

We crawled back through the tunnel and drove back to the embassy through the dark streets, arriving in the early hours of morning. The next day, I flew on to Prague. At the World Council of Churches I had met the Czech delegate, Professor Joseph L. Hromodka, head of the Faculty at the Protestant Seminary in Prague. We had talked at lunch, and he invited me to stay with him when I came to his country. We had three days to talk about his life under communist rule. He explained that he agreed with communism's endeavor to establish the brotherhood of man, but he disagreed with their view of humanity, that man was merely a unit in a group. He believed in man's individual transcendent reality as the object of God's love and did not believe that an earthly paradise would result from the realization of the communist objective.

He was followed everywhere he went by the secret police of the dictatorship that had robbed the people of their liberty while trying to preserve the outward appearance of freedom. He said freedom was replaced by the slavery of factory workers, peasants, and religious leaders. Dr. Hromodka added that the secret police even attended every church service. As long as the sermon was about personal prayer, life after death, or the sufferings of Jesus, it would be ignored, but any mention of the regime or its actions and the pastor might never be heard from again.

As I prepared to leave Poland and Czechoslovakia behind, I offered a simple prayer of thanksgiving for the United States of America, a reality, not a hopeless dream, an embodiment of democracy—the most desirable form of government. Our government is not perfect or complete, but the Constitution allows it to strive to be.

Displaced Persons and the Deaconesses

I hope I have not given the impression that most acts of kindness cost nothing and take little effort. Some are like that, but most require us to dig into our spiritual resources and often our wallets. This is how it should be. Christ did not come to benefit from our surplus but to change our roots. I would be reminded of this when I returned from Prague to Frankfurt, on a Swiss airline, to meet a group of nine other pastors. We had received permits to be the first civilian group to tour postwar Germany. We gathered at the Palmengarten Hotel where our two buses were waiting. One bus would be filled with food and the other would carry us through five major cities: Frankfurt, Stuttgart, Ulm, Munich, and Nuremberg. Every block of every city exhibited the destruction of war—piles of rubble that had once been stores and houses, schools and factories. In places, it seemed as if houses had been singled out as targets for bombing. Ulm was almost leveled; only the tall spire of the cathedral still stood above the ruins. In this city, we saw men, women, and children living in holes in the ground and niches in the rubble.

Starving people watched us through the windows when we sat to eat our meal in our hotel in Munich. Unable to eat, we carried our plates outside to them and scraped the food into their outstretched hands. In Nuremberg, we attended sessions of the War Crime trials. In Stuttgart, we spent two days working with local organizations handing out bowls of porridge to the thousands of displaced persons, known as DP's. Nazis had captured these people and brought them to Germany to work in the factories during the war. When the war was over, they were unwilling to return home to Estonia, Latvia, Poland, Czechoslovakia, and East Germany to live under communist rule. So they were homeless, desperate, and stranded in DP encampments. I promised myself that I would do something to help when I got back to Toledo.

I also discovered a shining ray of hope in the work of the deaconesses, in hospitals, homes, and churches. I had seen nothing like them in the U.S. I asked if, like nuns, they were forbidden to marry, but found that there were no such rules. Most of them were just young women with a deep sense of call to dedicated Christian service, paid only in gratitude and a small stipend for expenses. We visited a Deaconess Mother House, one of the finest hospitals. At what used to be another hospital, we saw twelve young women laboring with the workmen in the rubble, picking out and removing usable bricks from the debris. One of my American friends whispered that he would not do that for a million dollars. A deaconess heard him and responded, "Neither would we!" Not for money were they doing this rough work and singing rather than sighing.

At the end of our two-week tour, we met Bishop T.W.E. Sommer, a gray-haired, kindly man of vast learning, great administrative ability, and immense personal charm. He was an excellent interpreter of postwar German mentality and one of the three Methodist bishops in Europe. His area covered the whole of Germany—320 pastors and 110 deaconesses. We asked him what was the future of racial discrimination in Germany. He answered, "What Americans and most Europeans don't understand is that Hitler was the most un-German man in our history. He is the epitome of all that most Germans are not. Through all the years of oppression, not one true German approved. Americans do not think of Germany before 1933. Hitler and his maniacs did not represent our long history as one of the kindest and most peaceful nations in Europe."

"How then do you explain Hitler's election?"

"Hitler was a product of German despair. If the Allies, after World War I, had given Germany half the concessions that they gave to Hitler, then he would never have come to power. People said, 'What can we lose?' When they found out, it was already too late. Hitler's secret police had a stranglehold that made escape impossible. In any case, if Germany is permitted to regain her freedom and recover her characteristic life, it will be the farthest extreme from Nazism; she will prove herself to be a friend of all Europe. If the Allies do not destroy Germany, then her economic life, with adequate safeguards, will have a chance to assist in the formation of the United States of Europe."

My Immigrants:
Six Couples and Alma

In the DP camp, I promised to help fourteen to immigrate to Toledo, Ohio, and to provide them with both housing and employment. I also committed myself to help the Methodist Church in Zuffenhausen. (I also sent back money to provide teachers and a school for the children of the DPs.) The governors of the DP camp required passage money for the DPs from Germany to Toledo. I would have to raise that as well as finding houses and jobs—seven homes and seven jobs for seven couples. (I had to specify married couples with no children.)

Finding homes would not be too hard, but Toledo was a strong union town, and finding jobs would be tough. I gave interviews to the newspapers about the dire conditions in postwar Germany, and the unacceptable option of

the DPs returning home to their native countries, now sti-
fled under communism. As a result, I received many invitations to speak to churches, social clubs, service clubs,
even PTAs and union meetings. I accepted every invitation
on the condition that I could take a freewill offering after
my speech. Within two months, I had raised $8,000. Now
I could inform the camp directors that I had passage
money, and I already had the housing—rented apartments.
The union leaders promised me ten jobs, for six couples
and one single woman, a nurse 28 years of age. They were
among the first DPs from Eastern Europe to arrive in
America.

A community committee was organized to help our DPs
become acclimated to their new surroundings and lives.
We had to provide clothes and everything they would
need; they brought nothing from their former lives. It was
a stimulating experience for the entire community. The six
couples were soon settled, but the 13th person was something special. She came with papers and even spoke a little
English. A church family took her in until we could find a
job for her. I went to the local hospital to seek employment
for her. It took me a week to persuade the superintendent
of nurses to give her a chance.

It was a great day when Alma put on her nurse's uniform. The State Board of Nursing had waived all waiting
periods because of the excellent record recounted in her
papers. The nurses prepared a room for her in the Nurse's
Home and put flowers on the table. We had a party. Then,
they told Alma that she would have a tour of the hospital
to see their methods. All the newspapers featured her
story; everyone watched and waited for Alma to start

work. On the hospital tour, the next day, Alma was walking down the hall with the superintendent just as some orderlies brought a patient out of surgery headed for the recovery room. The patient's face was bloody and the smell of the anesthesia still hung in the air. Alma took one look at the patient and fainted. The nurses picked her up, put her in a bed, and began to tend to her. Alma's papers were forged. She had no training as a nurse; we were all shocked and dismayed. Alma and I met with hospital personnel and told them of the terrible conditions that Alma had fled. Eventually, they understood her desperation and, after they got acquainted with her, forgave her. They found a position that she could fill and got on with their lives.

Lastly, with my copious notes and ample memories, I called on Grove Patterson to make a report of my adventure. When he heard about the Polish colonel, my interrogator, he said we must go to the university he claimed to attend and check his story. We made an appointment with the president of the institution and went to see him. The colonel had indeed been enrolled and attended the school as he had claimed. In his file was a notification that he had been asked to leave for chronic absenteeism. A note read: "We suspect that this young man is visiting Detroit, Cleveland, Chicago, etc., and taking pictures. We found much photographic equipment in his dormitory room after he left."

Photographic materials owned by a foreign national in time of war were certainly cause for suspicion. The president asked, "May I have your word that you will not name this institution in any story you tell?" We both promised never to tell and have both kept our word. As we left the campus, I decided that I had had enough of being venture-some, but that I was grateful for the experience.

Dr. Albert Schweitzer

It was July of 1950 when I arrived in New York for a week of lectures at Columbia University. I had no sooner registered at my hotel than the desk clerk handed me a message from a former Yale classmate, Jerry Walker. The note read: "Emergency. Phone me immediately." Jerry worked in the Mayor's office and I could not imagine what he might need me for. It was about nine o'clock and registration started at eleven, but Jerry's note urged me to skip settling in and call him. "Howard," he exclaimed, sounding relieved. "I need you here at the Waldorf Astoria at eleven o'clock this morning."

I protested, "Jerry, I can't be there this morning. I'm registering for lectures. Can't we make it tomorrow?"

"No, you must come today! If you don't, you will regret it for the rest of your life."

This all sounded a bit melodramatic to me, but I had known Jerry for a long time, and great mysteries were not his style. Obviously, he had something really important on his mind, but was the mystery compelling enough to make me late for the lectures? I was the curious sort and had to admit that I was intrigued. "What is this all about?" I asked.

"I can't," Jerry pleaded, "It's secret. Just please come."

"You win. I'll come."

"Wonderful," he cried, sounding absolutely thrilled. "You will never regret it." Then he gave me directions for gaining access to the hotel that seemed as mysterious as the visit itself. I was truly mystified by the time I boarded the subway to Times Square. As I approached the Waldorf, I could see that something unusual was going on. A crowd had gathered in front, making it impossible to get in. As Jerry instructed, I dodged the crowd and went around the hotel to the service entrance. Jerry met me there and led me to an elevator, which we rode to the Roof Garden. Tables for 50 to 75 people were set close together, decorated with flowers and set with the distinctive Waldorf china, silver, and crystal.

As Jerry and I joined the receiving line, I suddenly caught sight of the object of all this attention. No one could ever mistake this giant of a man who stood head and shoulders above the rest of us. I remembered reading that he was in the United States but not that he would be in New York. He commanded an impressive audience—the receiving line included the Mayor of New York, the Vice-

President of the United States, military brass, university presidents, and other notables. Jerry had been right; I never would have forgiven myself if I missed my chance to meet Dr. Albert Schweitzer.

Waiters were spreading out a magnificent luncheon as Jerry and I approached the head of the receiving line where Dr. and Mrs. Schweitzer stood under a green canvas awning. They had come to the United States to speak at Westminster College in Fulton, Missouri, and were just passing through New York. This would be their only trip to the United States.

I had always admired Dr. Schweitzer. Here was a man who had reached the top of the musical world as a master organist and one of the greatest interpreters of the music of Johann Sebastian Bach. He had been educated in Universities in Strasbourg, Berlin, and Paris. He might have lived comfortably in wealth and style, but instead he chose to serve the poor and sick people in a village in Africa as a missionary doctor. He was one of the greatest humanitarians of the twentieth century.

Dr. Schweitzer towered over the people who were coming toward him in the receiving line. I found it interesting that this mental and moral giant should be a physical giant also. He had an enormous head, which was topped by a great shock of white hair, and a walrus mustache, also white. He appeared to have great physical strength, and I wondered if he would crush my hand when he shook it. But, despite his appearance, he was gentle, and I saw a radiance in his face and a light in his steel-gray eyes.

"I am happy to meet you," he said, as I placed my hand in his. His wife, standing next to him, was a complete contrast, petite and soft-spoken. I marveled at their differences.

Ever the enterprising one, Jerry had managed to get us seats directly across the table from the guests of honor; I was very pleased by this arrangement. I intended to enjoy every minute and pay attention to every word of Dr. Schweitzer's, as I could not expect this privilege again. Many important and distinguished guests stood to tell us in speeches how much they admired the guest of honor. I could see Mrs. Schweitzer having trouble staying awake through the drawn-out production, and I thought to myself how much she must miss the relative quiet of the jungle. Finally all the speakers sat and the man we had come to hear stood. I wish I could quote every word he said. I sat enthralled by the man, his life, and his words. What he said went something like this:

"Only those who respect the personality of others can be of real use to them. I think, therefore, that no one should compel himself to show to others more of his inner life than he feels is natural to show. We can do no more than let others judge for themselves what we inwardly and really are, and do the same ourselves with them. The only essential thing is that we strive to have the light in ourselves. Others will recognize our strivings, and, when people have light in themselves, it will shine out from them. Then we get to know each other as we walk together in the darkness, without needing to pass our hands over each other's faces or intrude into each other's hearts."

He also spoke of his personal philosophy, "reverence for life"—his theory of the universe, which ran counter to the spirit of the age and expressed his belief that we should respect life in all its forms. I sat as if spellbound during his entire speech, because his aura and presence were so great. And as he neared the end, his words imprinted themselves in my mind.

"The mistake most of us make," he said, "is thinking that with so many responsibilities at home and in business, with our noses forever to the grindstone, there is no chance for us to do good in the world. Take on yourself a second job, a vocation of helpfulness to people. There is no pay except the privilege of doing so. But in this job there will be wonderful opportunities—a deep strength and blessing for both the giver and the receiver. Your first vocation makes a living, your second makes a life." There it was— acts of kindness, in spades.

The luncheon ended shortly after his speech concluded. As Jerry and I rode the elevator back down to the street— he to his job at the Mayor's office, I to my lectures—he turned to me with a look of awe on his face. "Two jobs," he repeated. "One makes a living, and one makes a life. Do you realize that Dr. Schweitzer has just given us the secret of happiness?"

General Norstad and Ambassador Harriman

Some people are so genuinely courteous and helpful that their whole lives seem to be endless streams of acts of kindness. I used to think that such beings were scarce in high places, but on my first Sunday at The American Church in Paris I was happily proven wrong. On the previous Wednesday, Arthur Limorise, the young associate pastor, had asked me to do him a special favor—to conduct the service without him. He had been on duty for four months without a break and hoped that he and his wife could take a holiday trip that weekend. I had had enough experience to feel confident, so I told him to go ahead, even though Dr. Clayton Williams, pastor of this church, had assured me that his associate would always be there to introduce me and help with the service.

There was only one problem with me serving alone. It was the custom of this church for the minister to stand at the door after the service to greet the parishioners. I told Arthur this could cause a difficulty because, "I never learned the meaning of the insignia worn on the uniforms of our servicemen, and I won't know how to address them."

"That could be a problem," Arthur answered, "but it is very easy to deal with. If the serviceman is young, then give him the benefit of the doubt and call him 'captain.' If he is older, than just address him as 'colonel.' Many captains, majors, and colonels come to church here."

I was relieved by his simple solution to my problem and wished him a happy holiday. We had a fine service with outstanding music and great congregational participation. After the service I went to the door and began to shake hands with people as they went out. I addressed the young officers as "captain" or "major" and the line was moving along without a hitch. Near the end of the line, a tall man with an attractive wife and a teenage daughter approached me, followed by a number of military people who looked like NATO personnel. The tall man had gray hair and so I gave him my hearty greeting: "Good morning, Colonel."

Everybody in the group began to smile, snicker, and even laugh out loud. The tall man bent down and whispered in my ear, "The name is Norstad, and I'm a general."

Can you imagine my reaction? Embarrassment sent my face through every shade of red from blush to beet. I apologized at least three times, but he said, "Don't worry about it, I haven't been a general for too many years." Then he introduced his wife and daughter.

That, however, was not the end of the story. The following Wednesday, Colonel Collins telephoned from NATO. General Norstad had asked him to invite me to spend Friday with him and to have a tour of NATO. He added that if I could be ready by eleven o'clock, a car would be waiting at the front door of my apartment.

At first I said, "Oh, no! I'm not taking any chances of being imprisoned by General Norstad."

Colonel Collins laughed at my response and said, "No danger, we've all been calling him 'Colonel' behind his back and have had a really lively week."

I agreed to the visit, and Friday, at eleven o'clock, a NATO car appeared. I spent the day with General Norstad and his staff, and he couldn't have been nicer. He told me about his father who was the pastor of a Lutheran church in Minnesota, and we had a pleasant lunch in his office. The most impressive thing about that office was the size of the desk. I could never have imagined such a desk! And running across the front of it was a row of buttons—all alike, except for the last one, which was inlaid in pearl. He smiled at me and began to explain the buttons.

"The first one calls Colonel Collins. The second is for the West German Commander. The third is the American Commander. The fourth is the French and the fifth, the British." He went on to explain the purpose of several other buttons, including one that opened a direct line to the White House, but he did not mention the one inlaid in pearl. That one piqued my curiosity, so I asked about it.

"Well, that's a button we don't use."

I persisted, "Well, what do you mean you 'don't use' it?"

"Dr. Mumma, if I pressed that button, then a lot of activity would take place. It would involve all of Western Europe." This comment made me decide it would be best to abandon that part of the conversation.

During my tour, Colonel Collins briefed me on all the various insignia worn by the servicemen at NATO. My Sunday embarrassment had made me a fast study, and I memorized each and every one—since that day I have been able to successfully identify them all and can even recite them at will. After my tour was complete, I returned to the church very pleased with my day.

Another memorable Sunday meeting occurred during the Korean conflict. Looking out over the full congregation, I recognized Ambassador Averell Harriman. He was in Paris with the people who were trying to find ways to begin negotiations to end that troubling conflict. He appeared very attentive during the service, and I was disappointed when after the service he said, "Sir, I did not understand a word of your sermon; I could hear the music, but not your words. My hearing aid and your amplifying system are certainly on two different wavelengths. I would like to have a copy of your sermon if you have it. I noticed, however, that you did not use notes, and if you do not have it written out in manuscript form, that's perfectly all right. But, if you should have it, then I would be happy to send a messenger for it."

I answered, "Sir, I do have it in manuscript, in my study. If you can wait one moment, I will get it for you."

Ambassador Harriman answered, "Better still, why don't you bring it tomorrow, noon, and join me for luncheon?"

I liked that idea. The next day, I took my sermon to the American Embassy and enjoyed a fine lunch. I also had the honor of meeting some of our State Department people who were assisting in the effort to bring North and South Korean dignitaries to the negotiating table. When I was expressing my thanks, Ambassador Harriman said, "Any time you want to come here to the personnel dining room, for luncheon or dinner, you are welcome."

I accepted this offer three or four times a week. It was the only place in Paris that you could get a real American hamburger!

LESSONS

Death and Kindness

We seldom associate death with kindness. Yet there is seldom any greater need for kindness than when survivors grieve, especially children when they experience the loss of a parent, close relative, or dear friend for the first time. When I was five, my closest friend was Connie Allen. Every day we played together in the sand pile or rode our tricycles up and down the sidewalks. We planted and took care of a small flower garden. All my experiences were shared with Connie. One day, though, she could not play with me; her mother said she was sick. The next day was the same, and then she was not in Sunday school. A few days later, my father told me that Connie had died; God had taken her away to live with him. I asked myself, "What kind of good God would do that?"

My mother and father took my brothers and me to visit the Allen family. Connie was lying under a beautiful, white blanket in a fancy white box, with her eyes closed. The next day we went to the funeral and the minister again talked about the "good" Lord who took Connie away to live with him. I did not pray again for a long time. I wanted no part of a God who would take away my best friend. I needed someone to lift me from my sadness, or at least to help me bear it, but no one did.

When I was a little older, I wondered why no one had interpreted death to me. There were lots of explanations about life and how to live, but no words about death. Be assured that at some time, all children need some such explanation. Parents might ask a question to find out what a child thinks about death. It might be profound and simple. It is important to realize that the way you feel is more important than what you say. If you show fear or strain, the child will perceive it and think death is a bad thing.

One answer to the child's question, "What happens after death?" might be the honest statement, "We do not know or understand it. It may be something we could not even imagine. But I believe God, who loves us now, will continue to love us." If God is love, we do not have to be anxious about what will happen to us. How I wish something like that had been said to me when Connie died.

A wise parent will build up the concept of the soul as separate from the body when children are still quite young. Point to the child saying, "Who is this?" If the answer is, "Me," then say, "That is the body-house you live in, but not the real you. You are inside, special, separate." Then if somebody close dies, the child may accept that the real person is still somewhere, not gone. We all share birth and death, and children experience both in their life's journey. Pearl Buck expressed the experience in *The Big Wave*:

> *Kino* (a child): What is death?
> *Father*: Death is the great gateway.
> *Kino*: The gateway—where?
> *Father*: Can you remember when you were born?
> *Kino*: I was too small.
> *Father*: I remember very well. Oh, how hard you thought it was to be born! You cried and you screamed.
> *Kino*: Didn't I want to be born?
> *Father*: You did not. You wanted to stay just where you were in the warm, dark, house of the unborn. But the time came to be born, and the gate of life opened.
> *Kino*: Did I know it was the gate of life?
> *Father*: You did not know anything about it so you were afraid of it. But see how foolish you were! Here we were waiting for you, your parents, already loving you and eager to welcome you.

That's it! That's what makes it possible for all of us, old and young, to face death with courage and hope. We do not know the details. There are surprises ahead, but through faith, we know that God is waiting for us at the gateway. This is a gift we need to share with our children.

The Teddy Bear

Jimmy was a freckle-faced, curly-haired, five-year-old with a clubfoot. He had been left on the doorstep of the orphanage when he was only a few days old. Nobody ever came to claim him, and nobody wanted to adopt him, because he had to use a crutch. So, he stayed at the orphanage. The good ladies who visited the children each Christmas had given him a big brown teddy bear. It became his best friend and constant companion. He carried that teddy bear everywhere and slept with it at night.

In good weather, he and his teddy bear would hobble just outside the dormitory to the baseball field together. Even though he couldn't play, he loved to watch. Sometimes the other boys would let him keep score, but most often he could only stand and watch, enjoying the good plays and silently wishing that he could join in the sport. One afternoon while enjoying a game, a bully grabbed Jimmy's teddy bear out from under his arm and threw it over the wall and into the street. Jimmy went as fast as he could out into the street to rescue his friend, and as soon as he bent to pick his bear up, a truck struck him, knocking him and his bear into the gutter.

An ambulance came and sped Jimmy, still holding tight to his bear, to the emergency room. The examining physician was a young intern who was finishing up his shift. After inspecting the injuries, the intern went to the elevator to ride up to his room. He was sad for the boy, and his face reflected his depression. Dr. Harvey Cushing, a world-famous surgeon, boarded the same elevator, accompanied by four assistant surgeons. Seeing the intern's expression, Dr. Cushing asked, "What is the matter with you? You look down in the dumps."

The intern responded, "Well, I have just seen a sad case. I have been examining a five-year-old from the Boston City Orphanage. A truck hit him, leaving him with a crushed shoulder, a broken left arm, and a few other injuries. The interesting thing about him is that, when he was brought in, he was holding a teddy bear that also had a crushed arm and a crushed leg as well. Both the arm and leg were flat and filthy with grease. Jimmy insisted that I examine the bear, before I examined him. The sad thing though is that the boy already had a clubfoot, and there's not a whole lot we can do for his injuries."

"Would you like me to have a look at him?" offered Dr. Cushing.

The intern's face lit up, "That would be wonderful!"

So the six of them rode the elevator back down to the emergency ward where Dr. Cushing proceeded to give Jimmy another thorough exam. Throughout it all, Jimmy lay quietly on his bed with his bear beside him. Finally, Dr. Cushing turned to one of his assistants saying, "Have this boy in my operating room tomorrow morning at seven o'clock."

The young intern was grateful and said, "I'll be there too, with the nurses."

Promptly at 7:00, the team assembled in the operating room and went to work setting and repairing the broken bones. When those injuries had been repaired, Dr. Cushing turned to Jimmy's clubfoot. They worked for another two and a half hours. They opened the foot and carefully scraped away the excess calcium, putting the foot back together so it was straight. Then they sewed it up and braced it, so that it would mend properly. Five and a half hours after starting, Dr. Cushing finally laid down his instruments. He said, "That's a job complete," and wiped his forehead.

Jimmy was wheeled back to the children's ward where he stayed for several weeks recovering. All the staff grew fond of him. He was so brave and uncomplaining. His bear may have heard him cry, but the nurses never did. When the day to leave came, he said goodbye to all his new friends and an ambulance carried him back to the orphanage. As the attendants carried him in, all his friends cheered and waved. "We're glad you're home!" they shouted. Jimmy and his bear were back in their own bed in the dormitory.

As the weeks went by, Jimmy worked hard to learn to walk again. One happy day, he walked out into the yard.

Before long came the triumph of walking without the crutches, balancing instead on two canes. After a few weeks, he walked without any extra support. By summer, he had learned to run a bit and knew it was time to play ball. He ran out into the field and a friend gave him a glove. Somebody else threw the ball at him, and he caught it. He had been watching so carefully for so long, that he instantly knew how to move. Every afternoon, from that day forward, Jimmy played catch with anyone who was not in the game. Finally on one glorious afternoon, he heard the words he had wanted to hear for so long, "C'mon Jimmy, you're on the team."

Jimmy's baseball skills steadily improved until he became a fairly good outfielder. One day, when his turn to bat came up, he hit a sharp line drive for a single. His next at bat, he made it all the way to third, and the next boy drove in the run. As Jimmy crossed the plate, scoring his first run, he knew true happiness, at last.

That night, Jimmy approached the superintendent of the orphanage. "Mr. Goodson, would you give me permission to go downtown to Boston tomorrow?"

It was against the rules, but something in the boy's eyes made the superintendent agree on the condition that Jimmy promised to come back early. Jimmy promised, saying, "I only have one errand, and then I will come straight back."

The next day, instead of playing baseball, Jimmy dressed neatly and, carrying his teddy bear under his arm, boarded the bus heading to the Medical Arts Building. When he arrived, boy and bear rode the elevator to the tenth floor where all the nurses recognized him and greeted him.

"Jimmy, you look wonderful. You are all healed up and walking as if you never needed a crutch!"

Jimmy asked one of the nurses, "May I see Dr. Cushing, please?"

"He's in today. I'll see if he can see you." The nurse trotted off to find the doctor and quickly returned, saying, "He said he could see you right now."

"Come in!" Dr. Cushing said when Jimmy knocked on the door. As Jimmy walked in, the doctor stood up and came around his desk to shake Jimmy's hand. "I'm glad to see you. How are you?"

Jimmy had a very serious look on his face when he replied, "I have come to pay my debt." Then he continued, "This is all I have," handing the teddy bear to Dr. Cushing, "it's yours."

Dr. Cushing held the bear in his arms. Its arm and leg were still crushed and greasy from the accident. Carrying the bear, he went over to the window and, looking out over Boston Harbor, thought for a moment. Then he walked back to Jimmy, still cradling the teddy bear lovingly in his arms. "Thank you very much. Your bill is paid in full. I'm glad you are well and walking."

They shook hands and Jimmy returned to the orphanage.

Dr. Cushing died some years ago, but his former patients still tell an interesting story about him. Everyone who ever entered his reception room remembers the table in the center of the room—on it was a specially constructed glass case containing a battered teddy bear and a handwritten card that read, "This is the highest fee I ever received for an operation."

Said Jesus, "I tell you the truth: unless you change and become like little children, you will never enter the kingdom of heaven."(Matthew 18:3–4) At one time I interpreted this verse as a praise of innocence. I was very wrong. How many of us, as adults, are willing to part with our last prized possession in gratitude for a gift of kindness to which no strings were attached?

The Shadow of Influence

I could go on at length recounting my experiences as a parish minister, but instead I prefer to summarize the principal lesson that gradually came to dominate my outlook. I came to see that acts of kindness display perhaps the greatest influence we can ever hope to exert. Still, underlying this is the general influence that the sum total of our lives exerts. Think of it as a shadow. Everyone casts a shadow of influence that either blesses or blights, hurts or heals. You can no more keep from exerting your influence than you can keep from casting a shadow on a sunny day. Put another way, just as you cannot throw a stone into a pool without causing ripples that reach out in ever widening circles until they reach the shore, you cannot fit your personality into the sphere of life without causing ripples of influence that widen out until they lap on the shore of eternity. There is an ancient Jewish proverb that says, "He who saves one life, in time saves mankind." Taken literally, the words are hyperbole, but taken spiritually, they state a basic truth. Jesus saw this in the widow's mite. Unfortunately, we do not think often enough about the waves of influence emanating from us; silent, invisible, powerful forces that affect other people's lives, shape their opinions, and mold their thoughts, lifting them up in inspiration or pulling them down to the depths of despair. We know that we all are tremendously influenced by these shadows—by what other people say, do, or think—yet we rarely think about how we affect others.

For example, during a parent–teacher discussion of delinquency, a concerned teacher suggested that a careful survey of the homes where delinquent children lived might uncover the cause of their delinquency. A parent rose in opposition to the suggestion, saying, "What we need to do is teach common honesty in the schools. My boy gets his pencils stolen here at school every day. No sooner does he lay his pencil down on his desk than somebody steals it. Of course, I'm not complaining about the pencils, they don't cost me anything. I work for the government and bring pencils from the office to keep him well supplied. But, if we could just teach a little common honesty at school, then we wouldn't need a survey."

The man stood there wondering why everybody was laughing. What child could miss that lesson by example? No lecture on stealing pencils from school desks could offset the silent, indirect education of that home and the influence of the father who saw nothing wrong in stealing pencils from the government.

A police lieutenant talked to our service club, citing a similar case. He said, "You are driving down the street, in excess of the speed limit, and you say, 'Son, keep your eyes peeled for cops.' If you discredit the law in the eyes of your son, do not be surprised if sometime he breaks the law and your heart."

Our influence contains the mysterious power of goodness, a power beyond measure. The poet Robert Browning was struck with the unconscious influence radiating from a single personality—one so socially obscure as to leave no apparent trace, yet wielding a lasting influence. The thought of this power gave rise to Browning's poem "Pippa Passes." It is the story of a little factory girl in Italy who goes up and down the hills of her village singing, "God's in his heaven, all's right with the world." Then Browning tells how the passing of this pure, innocent girl halts a pair of guilty lovers, stops an angry man from cold vengeance, clears the fevered brain of a fanatic preparing to assassinate a ruler, and restrains a worldly bishop from succumbing to temptation.

Endowing God With
Our Own Weakness

After a college chapel service, a number of students asked for private interviews, one by one. My schedule made it impossible, but I agreed to sit down with about twenty-five of them and answer their questions. During the course of my address, I had made several statements concerning the nature of God. I said that some of us believe that God is the creator of the universe. We think of God as active in history, sitting in judgment over civilizations, ordaining their rise and fall. But down through the centuries, people have believed something more about God—not only is he out there in nature and history, but he is also here, right now, active in our lives. God the spirit is an active, present force in human life. Unfortunately, this concept of God as an ever-present help in our inner lives is almost forgotten by people today.

Then a young man asked a question I never will forget: "Do you mean that just as God has a plan for the universe, he has a plan for each individual's life?" After a moment's thought, I said, "Yes, I do. Back in Biblical times, men believed that God had a plan for their lives. Shakespeare wrote of 'a divinity that shapes our ends, rough hew them as we will.' Many great men from the Bible age to the present have believed that they were instruments of the Almighty and that God had directed them in their work."

A young lady spoke up: "I'll grant that if I could believe that God had a purpose for my life it would make a difference in the way I lived, but it is hard for me to be convinced of that. I am so small, so insignificant. This world is only a speck in the universe we inhabit, and I am only a tinier speck on that. Perhaps God has a plan for the whole thing, but I find it hard to believe that he has a plan for me."

My reply was, "I think we can all sympathize with that point of view. After all, there are billions of people in the world. But, let us stop a moment and think. Are we endowing God with our own weakness? You and I may see purpose in the large but not in the small, yet it is there. God does not make people the way we make cars and refrigerators. He is interested in all his people, perhaps because we are all different—each of us is an original. The greatest man who ever lived said, 'Are not two sparrows sold for a farthing? One of them shall not fall to the ground without the Father knowing it. And even the hairs on your head are numbered.'"

Another student asked, "You said that God is active in human life—is active in our lives, here and now, for good. How shall we think of him?"

I answered, "It is possible that God is active in our lives by putting ideas in our minds. God implants his ideas for us in a mind willing to receive them."

I proceeded to tell them the story of a brilliant student named James Bashford. While at college in 1870, he became ill with typhoid fever, a dangerous disease in the days before modern sanitation and drugs. Even with the best nursing, his chances were not good, and he was past caring whether he lived or died. At the hour of crisis, he heard a voice speak to him, as if from a nurse close by: "Your work here is not yet done." It came with the authority of God himself. James raised his head. If God wanted him to go living, weak as he was, he would do it. From that hour, he began to get better and soon was restored to full energy and will.

He had not had hallucinations; he believed that God had spoken to him. The voice had spoken truly; he went on to become the president of Ohio Wesleyan University and an honored statesman of the church. It was his habit, while presiding over the university, to walk about the campus in the afternoons, making himself available to students who wished to talk to him. He was frequently asked, "I am not sure what to do with my life, do you have any suggestions to help me decide?"

Dr. Bashford would reply, "When the time comes to choose a vocation, I have three suggestions for you. First, find out for yourself what you really enjoy doing. Our likes and dislikes are good indicators of what we are fit for. We all tend to like the things we do well and dislike the things we do poorly. A boy who is forever tinkering, likes using his hands, shows that he would be happiest when his capacities and inclinations meet. He will be a productive mechanic, builder, or engineer. One who is a born trader, who would rather buy and sell than eat, will make a successful businessman—no good would come of trying to make him a professor. So, find what you like to do best.

"Second, ask your friends what they think you are fitted for. What do the people who know you best think about your capacities? What do your professors think? People who have nothing to gain or lose, what do they think you are good at? Ask the people who are not afraid to tell you the truth to your face. It helps us all to get a look at ourselves through other eyes. People do believe God speaks through our friends. We may be sure we are right for a certain career and find out that God is calling us to a different vocation, through our friends.

"Third, we need to ask: Where is the greatest need? God calls us through human needs also. Abraham Lincoln saw much slavery in his youth. It challenged him to his greatest work as the Great Emancipator. When Abe poled a raft down to New Orleans as a youth, he saw slavery at its worst, and promised himself that if he ever had the chance to destroy it, he would."

I ended my conversations with the young students by saying, "From my experience and from my study of great men and women in history, I think it is justified to think that God has a plan for you. If you want to know that plan, study your inclinations, consult your friends, investigate the present needs, then act by the light of the knowledge you have gained—in that way you will find his plan. When you find it, your life will be what it ought to be: helpful in its outreach, rich in its satisfactions, unwavering in your hours of decision, constant in trial, and rewarding in accomplishments. This is an act of kindness God bestows on us, if only we will use the resources and talents with which we are each endowed."

Bibliography

Buck, Pearl S. *The Big Wave*. New York: HarperCollins, 1986. 32–33.

Camus, Albert. *The Plague*. Translated by Stuart Gilbert. New York: Random House, 1948. 87, 117–118.

The Discourses of Epictetus. Translated by P. E. Matheson. Oxford: Clarendon Press, 1916. 179.

Lewis, C.S. *The Problem of Pain*. Glasgow: Fontane Books, 1957. 14.